SIMPLE
STRATEGIES

for Teaching Children

 K–5

I dedicate this book to two friends, Molly Stebbins and Lori Justice, who have been so critical in shaping my personal and professional life over the past 30 years.

—Melissa Stormont

With all of my love, I dedicate this book to my sons, Jake and Kevin Noah for becoming such good adults and for teaching me daily about life and what is really important.

—Cathy Newman Thomas

SIMPLE STRATEGIES

for Teaching Children

Melissa Stormont

Cathy Newman Thomas

CORWIN
A SAGE Company

CORWIN
A SAGE Company

FOR INFORMATION:

Corwin
A SAGE Company
2455 Teller Road
Thousand Oaks, California 91320
(800) 233-9936
www.corwin.com

SAGE Publications Ltd.
1 Oliver's Yard
55 City Road
London, EC1Y 1SP
United Kingdom

SAGE Publications India Pvt. Ltd.
B 1/I 1 Mohan Cooperative Industrial Area
Mathura Road, New Delhi 110 044
India

SAGE Publications Asia-Pacific Pte. Ltd.
3 Church Street
#10–04 Samsung Hub
Singapore 049483

Acquisitions Editor: Jessica Allan
Associate Editor: Kimberly Greenberg
Editorial Assistant: Cesar Reyes
Production Editor: Amy Schroller
Copy Editor: Linda Gray
Typesetter: Hurix Systems Private Ltd.
Proofreader: Stefanie Storholt
Indexer: Michael Ferreria
Cover Designer: Scott Van Atta

For information:

Printed in the United States of America

A catalog record of this book is available from the Library of Congress.

ISBN 978-1-4522-6841-5

This book is printed on acid-free paper.

MIX
Paper from
responsible sources
FSC® C014174

13 14 15 16 17 10 9 8 7 6 5 4 3 2 1

Contents

Acknowledgments

MELISSA STORMONT'S ACKNOWLEDGMENTS

I would like to thank two of my daughter's dedicated teachers. Taylor has characteristics that would place her at risk if she were not given support from home and school. Mrs. Lewis and Ms. Mathes are wonderful teachers who saw her strengths above her struggles and supported her in feeling good about herself. They also both contributed valuable information to the book. I also acknowledge my husband for being so supportive of this work.

CATHY NEWMAN THOMAS'S ACKNOWLEDGMENTS

I would like to thank Melissa Stormont for including me in the development of this book and for her very generous and skillful mentoring of my professional writing. And I want to thank my many teacher-friends across the years who have inspired my own teaching and research. From your dedication and passion, I have seen children at risk accomplish wonderful things that others doubted were possible, and together we continue to work to discover solutions to the challenges we experience in our teaching. With my deepest respect and admiration, I appreciate all that you do to improve the lives of children at risk.

PUBLISHER'S ACKNOWLEDGMENTS

Corwin gratefully acknowledges the contributions of the following reviewers:

Natalie S. McAvoy

Reading Specialist

Elkhorn Area School District

Elkhorn, WI

Susan Schipper

Elementary Teacher

Palmyra Public Schools

Palmyra, NJ

Barbara L. Townsend

Reading Specialist, West Side Elementary School

Adjunct Instructor, Concordia University

Elkhorn, WI

About the Authors

Melissa Stormont, PhD, is a professor in special education at the University of Missouri. She has published extensive research related to the educational and social needs of young children who are vulnerable for failure in school, including children with behavior problems, Attention Deficit/Hyperactivity Disorder, and children who are homeless. She spent three years as a preschool teacher and has spent years conducting field research in Head Start and elementary schools. The majority of her research efforts have focused on contributing factors to early behavior problems in young children. She has collaborated with many schools to build their capacity to better meet the needs of children at risk for failure. Dr. Stormont has published more than 75 articles, books, and book chapters related to the needs of children at-risk for failure. She is currently a co-principal investigator on a large-scale group randomized efficacy trial for a classroom management intervention funded by the Institute of Education Sciences (IES).

Cathy Newman Thomas, PhD, is an assistant professor in the Department of Special Education at the University of Missouri. She began her career as a special education teacher, practicing in California and New Jersey. She taught in self-contained special day classes, as a resource teacher, and as a coteacher. She was an educational consultant who conducted diagnostic evaluations to determine whether a student had a learning disability. During her 10 years as a teacher, she taught students from kindergarten through high school, including students in high-need urban areas and students consigned to a court-mandated drug rehabilitation center. She earned her doctorate from The University of Texas at Austin in 2008, with an emphasis in learning disabilities and behavior disorders. Her research focuses on technology in teacher education, technology to provide access to the curriculum for children at risk for school failure, and adolescent content area literacy, including digital literacy. Dr. Thomas has authored more than a dozen articles and has coauthored two book chapters. This is her first opportunity to co-author a book.

Introduction

The purpose of this book is to assist general educators in supporting the needs of children at risk for failure in school. Given that much of this information is not included in preservice education for general educators, it is very important that teachers have access to simple strategies to support children who are struggling. We also intend to provide systematic strategies general educators can use and to present them in an accessible manner. Teachers are incredibly busy, and we wanted to provide a guide that can be read over a weekend and used the following week in school. Our examples are hands-on and based on research. We begin by defining risk and how children's characteristics interact with school expectations to buffer or exacerbate risk. Then we present ways to support children at risk by building relationships in classrooms, collecting systematic data to monitor growth, stressing the importance of practice, implementing behavioral and academic interventions, using technology, and working with other professionals and families.

BOOK OVERVIEW

The approaches discussed in this book in Chapters 2 (building relationships) and 3 (data based decision making) are effective teaching strategies designed to meet the needs of all children and are especially important to use to address the needs of children at risk. Other strategies are particularly focused on increasing the success for children with increased needs for support. Chapter 4 includes the importance of increasing practice opportunities, Chapter 5 presents the social behavioral needs of children at risk for failure and Chapter 6 includes academic supports for children at risk. Chapter 7 includes a discussion of the importance of using technology to support children at risk for failure and ways teachers can utilize technology. In Chapter 8 we address the additional needs of increasing family involvement and collaboration across professionals for children at risk for failure.

1 Who Is at Risk for Failure?

★ When you consider your school, who do you think is at risk for failure?
★ When you think about risk for failure, do you think about both academic and social behavior failure?
★ How important do you think teachers are for preventing or reducing risk for failure?

Many children in schools today are at risk for failure (Stormont, 2007; Stormont, Reinke, Herman, & Lembke, 2012). Students who are at risk for failure include students who have within-child and/or within-environmental circumstances that put them in a vulnerable position for having problems in school (Kauffman & Landrum, 2009; Pianta, 1999; Pianta & Walsh, 1998; Stormont, 2007). These problems could be academic or social or both. Following are some specific statistics regarding risk factors:

★ Many children enter kindergarten at risk for failure due to limited skills, including academic and self-regulation skills (Stormont, Beckner, Mitchell, & Richter, 2005).
★ One in five children has social, emotional, and behavior problems (World Health Organization, 2004).
★ First-grade children with both academic and social behavior problems have the worst long-term outcomes compared with children with problems in one area only (Darney, Reinke, Herman, Stormont, & Ialongo, 2012; Reinke, Herman, Petras, & Ialongo, 2008).
★ If children with behavior problems maintain these problems into third grade, there is little chance they will ever not have behavior

problems; they will need substantial supports to be successful in school and life (Walker, Ramsey, & Gresham, 2004).

★ If children receive any mental health or social emotional interventions, they receive them in school (Hoagwood et al., 2007; Rones & Hoagwood, 2000).

★ Attention Deficit/Hyperactivity Disorder (ADHD) affects approximately 5% of school-age children; most children with ADHD spend the majority of the day in the general education classroom (Zentall, 2006).

★ Children with ADHD are at risk for a host of negative short-term and long-term outcomes, including social skill deficits, peer rejection, retention, low achievement, and dropping out (Stormont, 2001; Zentall, 2006).

★ Of individuals in this country, 15% meet the criteria for poverty (U.S. Census Bureau, 2012). Families are at increased risk for poverty as their incomes have declined (U.S. Census Bureau, 2013).

★ Individuals making minimum wage cannot afford a fair market apartment and often experience homelessness despite working full-time (National Coalition for the Homeless, 2009).

★ Approximately 37% of the homeless population includes families with small children (National Center on Family Homelessness, 2011).

★ Up to 1.6 million children experience homelessness each year in the United States (National Center on Family Homelessness, 2011). Children who are homeless are at great risk for academic and social problems in school (Davey, 2004; National Center on Family Homelessness, 2011; Stormont & McCathren, in press).

RISK AND RESILIENCE

According to systems theory and ecological theory, children interact with individuals in their environments and use experiences to direct future interactions with specific individuals and in certain settings (Kauffman & Landrum, 2009; Pianta, 1999; Stormont, 2007). Elementary school is a very important time for working to increase opportunities to build success for children at risk for failure (Stormont, 2007). Interactions with individuals in different environments can increase or maintain risk for failure or can be a place for fostering resilience through targeting needs for support (Kauffman & Landrum, 2009; Stormont, 2007).

In this chapter, specific within-child and within-environment characteristics that according to research are associated with risk for failure will be presented. Although there are theoretical frameworks that emphasize the community and additional levels of influence on children's resiliency, the focus of this book is on what general educators can directly impact to improve children's likelihood of success. Common characteristics and

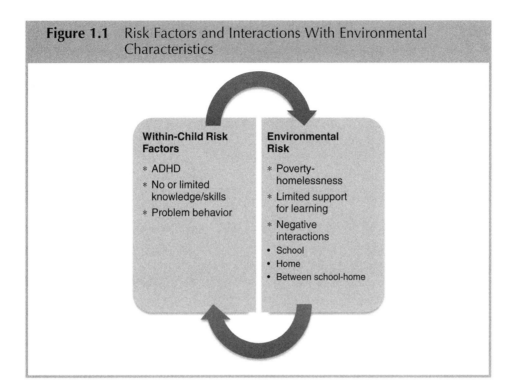

Figure 1.1 Risk Factors and Interactions With Environmental Characteristics

needs for support that children have will then be discussed. The framework used to conceptualize risk is the following from Stormont (2007):

1. Certain characteristics create risk for failure, including having negative social and academic outcomes.

2. Characteristics in children interact with characteristics in settings and increase or decrease risk for failure (see Figure 1.1).

3. Risk for failure does not mean failure is bound to occur.

4. Knowledge of risk characteristics should be used to inform needs for support.

CHILD CHARACTERISTICS

The children who are the focus of this book are those who do not have a disability but may be at risk for developing one without early intervention. The children targeted in this book are also those who are at great risk for falling through the cracks (Barkley, 2006; Espinosa, 2005; Zentall, 2006). The risk characteristics addressed in this book include the child characteristics of having ADHD, limited knowledge or skills related to academics and English, and behavior problems. Children with these risk factors have characteristics that create vulnerability for failure, particularly without early attention to their needs (Belfiore, Auld, & Lee, 2005; Coyne, Kame'enui, & Carnine, 2011; Espinosa, 2005; Herman, Reinke, Stormont, Puri, & Agarwal, 2010; Stormont, 2007; Walker et al., 2004; Zentall, 2006). Although children will have unique characteristics, there are some common characteristics that teachers need to understand and plan to support. These are discussed later in the chapter.

ENVIRONMENTAL CHARACTERISTICS

Family. Children from low-income backgrounds are at increased risk for failure (Belfiore et al., 2005; Espinosa, 2005). Poverty and homelessness have increased over the past several decades, especially within families, and teachers need to be responsive to the needs of children (Stormont & McCathren, in press). Children living in poverty are also at increased risk for one or more of the within-child characteristics presented earlier. An additional reason children who are poor and those who are homeless are at risk is that they move frequently. For example, as many as 97% of children who are homeless move in a given year (Paquette, 2011). Extensive instructional time is lost when children move, and teachers need to be prepared to use strategies presented in this book to closely monitor their progress. In addition, children will have specific characteristics that are more unique given their needs for resources and linkages with community agencies for supports (National Center on Family Homelessness, 2011). Their additional needs for collaboration with communities and other professionals to increase access to resources are addressed in Chapter 8. Parent involvement in school is a malleable risk factor associated with academic and social success and is also discussed in detail in Chapter 8.

School. Teachers often receive little preparation in their preservice education for addressing the needs of children at risk. Teachers report that they need more training in the area of supporting behavioral issues in the classroom (Reinke, Stormont, Herman, Puri, & Goel, 2011). Further, teachers often report inaccurate knowledge related to children with ADHD (Stormont & Stebbins, 2005). In recent survey research, the majority of educators (56%) did not agree with the statement "I am confident that the interventions and practices I use have the desired impact on the student" (Stormont, Reinke, & Herman, 2011a, p. 22). The lack of education and preparation for supporting children who are at risk for failure contributes to using inappropriate and ineffective strategies. This often leads to a negative interactive cycle between teachers and children and between teachers and parents, which is discussed next.

INTERACTIONS

Perhaps the largest factor contributing to risk for children is the lack of adult support. This is especially true if children have within-child characteristics that increase risk for failure and then are not supported in learning specific skills needed to be successful in different settings. When teachers and parents have expectations for children that children cannot meet, a negative interaction cycle begins (Stormont, 2007). Practices such as punishment without support for learning appropriate behavior and retention are common and not effective (Stormont, Lewis, Beckner, & Johnson, 2008). If children are not supported in succeeding and maintain academic and behavior problems into the third grade, their likelihood of ever being successful diminishes significantly (Stormont, 2007). This is referred to as the window of opportunity for early intervention, which closes almost completely by the third grade (Walker et al., 2004). The transition to kindergarten is a critical point of development that can increase risk for both academic and social behavior problems, especially when teachers have inappropriate expectations for children upon school entry (Stormont et al., 2005).

Interaction Examples. Espinosa (2005) describes the different outcomes for two cousins with limited English and the simple strategies one teacher used to make one student feel comfortable and the negative strategies another teacher used:

> Unintelligible noise is all that my cousin and I heard when we first heard English spoken to us. We clung together as we approached our school on the first day. I knew we would be all right as long as we stayed together. It never occurred to me that we would be separated and placed in different classes. Once I got over the terror at this event, I saw the friendly face of a person who held my hand and comforted me. She was my new teacher. She smiled and stayed close to me, making me feel more secure. My teacher taught me English when she could fit it into the day, sometimes over lunch. She taught me words in English and asked me to teach her words in Spanish. Once she learned some words and phrases, she taught them to the rest of the class. My new friends knew colors and how to count in Spanish, as well as basic greetings. They even learned my favorite song, "Los Pollitos." I would recite what I had learned in English and my classmates would clap for me. Sometimes we would get extra time at recess or a special activity because I had learned so many words in English and had taught

my classmates and teacher so much Spanish. My cousin had a very different experience. His teacher did not understand him, laughed at mispronounced words, and would not listen to him unless he spoke in complete sentences. He became angry and ashamed. He was sometimes punished for refusing to speak. Eventually he refused to cooperate on anything. (p. 838)

Stormont (2007) describes the failure cycle John experiences due to the interactions between his characteristics that put him at risk for failure and the responses of his teacher:

John rushes into class as the bell rings. His clothes are clean but crumpled and his zipper is unzipped. His first grade teacher expects students to be in the classroom when the bell rings, so he gets one check for this behavior. When children get three checks they miss recess. After the morning announcements and routines, the teacher asks the class to begin their writing work. A huge prompt on the board says "Writing work = Write about you" and has pictures and topics to help children generate ideas. John opens his desk to get out his folder for journal writing. He can't find it. As he removes large chunks of papers from his desk he is oblivious to the noise he is making. When he looks up, his teacher is standing over him with a disappointed look on his face. One more check. Then John remembers that his teacher keeps his journal because he keeps losing it. After he gets his journal he looks for something to write with. He can't find anything and begins asking his class-mates. Then he stands up and yells, "Hey does anyone have a pencil?" One more check. He has only been in school for one hour. Unfortunately it is a typical day for John. (p. 138)

In another example of how adults interact with children to increase or decrease risk for failure, Stacey Bess (1994) describes how she attempted to connect with children living in a homeless shelter and attending a school with no name. Her lack of understanding of the children's experiences is clearly illustrated in her introduction to the children:

"I'm Stacey," I began. "I brought along a little something to help you get to know me." I held up a scrapbook with "ME" pasted on the front cover. "This is my family," I explained as I opened the book to a picture of the four of us. "This is Greg, my cute husband. This is our daughter Nichole, and this is our little boy, Brandon." So far so good. Now I wanted to establish some common ground.

"My story starts with my three favorite likes, the three Cs: children, chocolate, and Coke—Diet Coke." As I stood there trying to convince them somehow that I could be one of them, that I could belong in their world, suddenly a mouse raced right across my feet. I jumped to the ceiling, screamed, and would have impressed Michael Jackson with my dance moves. My heart thumped in my throat as I gasped for breath and met the unblinking eyes of thirty kids staring at me in total disgust. (pp. 9–10)

If teachers feel they are in a negative interaction pattern with children and/or their parents, many simple effective strategies can be used to change this pattern. This book emphasizes (a) building positive relationships and on this foundation meeting children where they are, based on systematic data collection, and (b) teaching specific social and academic behavior to increase their success. Building positive relationships with families and other professionals is also important and discussed in Chapter 8.

Final case examples are provided by a primary-grade general educator who works very well with children at risk for failure and tries to foster resilience. She often loops with her students so she gets to work with them for two years.

Mrs. Lewis Fosters Resilience

I had a child some years back (in both first and second grade) who taught me a lot about working with kids who are at risk due to their home environment. Naya came from a family where one parent was in prison and the other had recently been released from prison. She lived with an ever-changing group of family members in quite poor conditions. Yet somehow Naya came to school every day with a smile on her face ready to learn. She went from not knowing what a book was in kindergarten to being above grade level in reading and *the* leader in the room in second grade. How? Because she said, "I'm going to be somebody."

I just soaked up everything Naya had to teach me about kids like her, and every year since, I have had opportunities to put it into practice with my other students who are at risk.

This year I have a student, Janie. Janie mostly raises herself and her small siblings and sees more than she should at home on a regular basis. Janie has no control in her life, and fighting for control in a safe environment like school helps to meet that need. Janie's behavior is a major obstacle, with several office referrals for bullying, fighting, disrespect, tantrums, and noncompliance. My plan of action with Janie from the beginning of the year:

★ Help her learn strategies for dealing with her emotions from home in appropriate ways
★ Help her to see herself as worthy
★ Help her see herself as a leader
★ Help her see herself as someone who will "be somebody"

We are three-fourths of the way through the year, and I feel like Janie is finally getting there. She has had two months straight without an office referral, and her tantrums have become nearly nonexistent. I take all the opportunities I can to tell Janie how smart she is. She is a beautiful girl, but at seven years old she needs to know she is more than beautiful. We talk about what she wants to do when she goes to college. Not *if* she goes to college. I try to pick specific qualities she has and point toward that helping her in a career. "Janie you are really great at explaining this math. Maybe you will go to college to be a teacher like me." I give Janie many opportunities to be a leader. Since Janie has very little control in her life, by giving her opportunities to help others, to lead a project, to volunteer for a kindergarten teacher, to organize something, I am giving her an opportunity to control something. I take out the emotion when dealing with consequences. "You made a poor choice, so you have to follow through with the consequences. Choose to learn from your mistake so it doesn't happen again. Tomorrow will be a better day." And very important . . ."I still love you even when you mess up."

I have little contact with this particular parent, but when I do talk to Janie's mom or any other parent of a child who is at risk I sing their praises. So often the parent is used to hearing that the kid is a behavior problem and they don't want to listen. I tell the parent about the problems, but I am sure to put three times as many positive things about the kid in there too. Also, I leave every conversation with a parent with this advice: "Tell her she is smart. Tell her she is going to college. Tell her she is going to be somebody. Tell her every day." At some point I hope that the kid will hear this in enough places in her life she'll begin to believe.

COMMON RISK CHARACTERISTICS

Children who are at risk for failure tend to share characteristics, but the reasons they have the characteristics may be different. For example, children with ADHD will display specific characteristics because of the way they process information and interact with the environment (Zentall, 2006). Children who are at risk due to limited experiences (e.g., because of poverty, homelessness, lack of stable education) will have similar characteristics, but it may be the result of a lack of the opportunity to learn and therefore to possess the prior knowledge required to be successful. For example, children at risk due to poverty enter kindergarten and may not have certain early language and literacy experiences (Espinosa, 2005), whereas children with ADHD may have had these experiences but may not have paid attention to the key features being discussed (Barkley, 2005). English learners with limited proficiency may exhibit characteristics similar to other students who are at risk, but their characteristics and needs are brought about by the process and demands of second-language acquisition as well as other risk factors they may face in their lives (Coyne et al., 2011; Espinosa, 2005; Stormont, 2007).

Children at risk for failure who are the focus of this book often have many of the following common characteristics:

- ★ **Attention problems.** Children may have a hard time coming to attention, focusing their attention on the right thing, and sustaining their attention.
- ★ **Impulsivity.** Children may have a hard time waiting their turn and taking turns. Children who are impulsive blurt out answers and have problems with thinking before acting.
- ★ **Hyperactivity.** Some children are more active than others and need to move more. Activity needs can be met through increasing opportunities to talk and physically move.
- ★ **Memory problems.** Children may have problems working with information long enough to get it to their long-term memories. Children may also have problems retrieving information from their long-term memories when needed.
- ★ **Limited motivation.** Children may not be engaged and interested in learning in general or learning specific things. Children may not see how things relate to them or may be more focused on other things that are troubling them. If children have limited skills in a specific area, they will probably be less motivated in that area. If the task is challenging, they may need an incentive to complete the task.
- ★ **Organization problems.** Children with organization problems often struggle in two areas of organization. One area is object organization, which includes knowing where their things are, bringing back homework, and having needed supplies for class. Children with object organization problems lose things frequently and often don't develop routines that other children develop to become more organized (Zentall, Harper, & Stormont-Spurgin, 1993). Children with organization problems also often struggle with time/planning

organization and need support managing complex projects and tasks such as those that are long term or have multiple steps, processes, and components (Zentall, 2006).

★ **Limited knowledge/skills.** Children with limited knowledge of English or with limited knowledge of academic content need support to more fully participate in class lessons and activities (Coyne et al., 2011; Espinosa, 2005; Stormont, 2007). Understanding where children are in terms of their knowledge and skills is critical for providing this support.

★ **Problem behavior.** Teachers most frequently report concerns related to disruptive behavior in elementary classrooms (Reinke et al., 2011). However, children often have other problem behaviors as well, including aggression, noncompliance, and internalizing behaviors such as being withdrawn, anxious, or depressed. Children with problem behaviors are at great risk for peer rejection and academic failure. Children need support in learning more socially appropriate ways to interact in their environments.

★ **Increased need for positive parent-teacher involvement.** Children who are at risk for failure need teachers and parents to work more closely to support their social, emotional, and academic success. Chapter 8 addresses this topic.

SUMMARY

★ In schools today, many children are at risk for failure.

★ Children who are the focus of this book are those who tend to fall through the cracks.

★ Children with ADHD, limited knowledge and skills, and problem behavior are at increased risk for failure.

★ Family and school environments interact with children's characteristics and increase or decrease children's risk for failure.

★ Teachers need to focus on common characteristics and build their ability to provide supports to lessen risk.

2 Strategies for Building Relationships

Bullying and other forms of maltreatment are less likely to occur in classrooms with strong communities (Jones & Jones, 2001). As Jones and Jones state, "An ounce of prevention is worth a pound of cure" (p. 75). When teachers model acceptance and explicitly teach their students that no one is left out and no one gets picked on, children feel safe being who they are (Jones & Jones, 2001). Also, when problems or disagreements arise, classrooms with strong communities respond better to these challenges. However, with the push for higher achievement scores, some teachers may rush to get started without taking time to build relationships in the classroom. Teaching academics and managing behavior will not be as effective without a background context of strong relationships (Jones & Jones, 2001; Stormont, 2007). From the first day of school, with students of all ages, teachers need to use time to build community and get to know their students. Students also need support to get to know each other.

This chapter includes the foundational classroom management principle of establishing positive relationships in classrooms. The chapter presents simple strategies teachers can use to build positive relationships with children within and outside the classrooms. Strategies for supporting positive relationships among children are also discussed.

Teachers can build relationships with students by doing the following (Dalton & Watson, 1997; Jones & Jones, 2001; Lehr & Christenson, 2002; Stormont, 2007; Watson & Ecken, 2003; Weinstein & Mignano, 2003):

★ Get to know each student, including learning names and preferred nicknames as soon as possible.

★ Get to know each student's likes, dislikes, and so on (see Table 2.1 for examples).
★ Be proactive by knowing children's individual needs for support.
★ Spend time with children—even for short periods—to get to know children, including their interests, preferences, and families.
★ Journal with children regarding likes, dislikes, and shared interests.
★ Greet and dismiss children with warmth and kindness.
★ Hold class meetings to determine class climate and if there is any need for discussion of specific topics.
★ During class meetings and throughout the day and year, model effective problem solving with students.

Teachers can also build relationships with students by collaborating with students regarding class rules and routines. One way to do this, described by Ms. Mathes (personal communication, February 2013), is to develop a *Wordle.* A Wordle is a graphic word cloud. Wordles are created using free online software available at http://www.wordle.net. When Ms. Mathes enters text, the Wordle program organizes the information by making the highest-frequency words stand out using text features such as size, style, and color. She is able to control such features as the font, font size, and color scheme. She can edit the Wordle to add or delete words, and a word count is available. A number of other similar programs are also available on the Internet. In making her Wordle, Ms. Mathes noted, "This year I put chart paper up with questions such as these:

★ What do we need to do to make this class run smoothly?
★ What do we need to do so everyone is happy in class?
★ What can the teacher do to help you learn?
★ What can you do to help yourself be a better learner?

Students went around the room and wrote their answers under each question in one or two words. Then I made a Wordle of their responses. Responses that students said a lot then became bigger in the Wordle. The Wordle is displayed in our classroom." Having the Wordle displayed helps Ms. Mathes and her students focus on the main ideas from their discussion (Stormont, 2007).

Build positive relationships among students by doing the following (Jones & Jones, 2001; Watson & Ecken, 2003; Weinstein & Mignano, 2003):

★ Have peers interview each other on specific topics.
★ Have peers share personal objects, ideas, or other relevant information.
★ Teachers can use the information on relationships to demonstrate math concepts, written expression, and reading. (How many students like to play soccer? Is that more or less than the number who like ice cream? Which person said something that surprised you? Who do you have something in common with?)
★ Student matches. Students can be assigned to find peers who have a particular characteristic and then get their signatures. An example

Table 2.1 Getting to Know You

I am left-handed X _____	My family likes to camp X _____	I am the oldest child X _____
I love to read X _____	I like ice cream X _____	I love to play soccer X _____
I am an only child X _____	I am involved in sports X _____	I have a pet X _____

is presented in Table 2.1. Teachers can modify this by including pictures for younger children.

★ Guess who? Students write down a fact about themselves and give it to the teacher. When the teacher reads the fact out loud to everyone, students have to guess who it is about. This can also be called "What is special about me?" or "Unique facts about me."

★ Fact and fiction. Students write one or two statements that are true about themselves and one that is false. Students guess which statement is false. This could be adapted and called "True or false."

★ Consensograms. Consensograms are a great way to use children's prior knowledge, helping them to connect their daily lives to the curriculum (Torres-Velasquez & Lobo, 2004–2005). The teacher hangs large sheets of paper across the classroom with questions and responses on them. Students are then given sheets with dot stickers and go around the room placing their dots under the responses they agree with the most. This is a super way for children to get to know each other, and it provides the teacher with a lot of information about their students. Sample questions include the following:

- What is your favorite reward (see Figure 2.1 for sample responses)?
- What is your favorite subject in school?
- How do you like to work (e.g., alone, with one person, with the teacher, etc.)?
- How many people are in your family?
- What is your favorite animal?
- What is your favorite activity?

Figure 2.1 What is Your Favorite Reward?

INTERVIEWING TO BUILD COMMUNITY AND QUESTIONING SKILLS

Ms. Castillo knows that her students struggle to formulate good questions, yet she realizes that interviewing each other will be a fun and also motivating way for her students to get to know each other and build the caring classroom community she desires. Fortunately for Ms. Castillo's students, she participated in professional development through the Integrated Curriculum Project and has planned an activity that will help her to meet her goals for her students (see Rieth et al., 2003; Thomas et al., 2012).

First, Ms. Castillo models the activity. She has brought a lunch bag from home with three personal objects in it that can help her students learn more about her. She has brought a picture of an elderly couple, a rock, and a DVD. She tells the children that they are going to learn to know her better, and also, they are going to learn to ask great research questions so that they will become researchers themselves! She holds up the first object, the picture, and she asks the children, "Who has a question about why this object is important to me?" Her students begin to raise their hands. Ms. Castillo calls on a student, Noah, who asks, "Do you know those people in that picture?" Ms. Castillo smiles at Noah, nods her head, and says, "Yes!" She waits expectantly for another hand to go up. Cassie has raised her hand, and when called upon, she asks her teacher, "Is that an old picture?" Again, Ms. Castillo nods and smiles and says, "Yes!" She prompts the students, "Can anyone think of a question that would make me give a longer answer?" Adrian raises his hand and asks, "Who are those people?" Ms. Castillo responds, "They are my grandparents." Now, more hands go up! Questions begin to flow, and now most would require an elaborated response. For example, Shaniqua asks her teacher, "Can you tell me about your grandparents and why you brought this picture?" Many enthusiastic questions follow, and Ms. Castillo's students are laughing and interacting as they learn about her family and their immigration from Mexico.

After this guided practice with the first object, Ms. Castillo reveals her next object, the rock, and begins a new round of practice in asking "good" questions that will result in the most information. Ms. Castillo is helping her students learn to distinguish and ask high-level questions about content through this interview activity. Tomorrow, each student will bring his or her own objects (or drawings or pictures of the objects) to share. Ms. Castillo will put the children into small groups of three. In these small groups, her students will have roles. One will be the *question asker,* one will be the *responder,* and one will be the *recorder.* They will each perform each role so that all her students have an opportunity to share about themselves, practice asking good questions, and in the role of recorder, serve as the group leader by taking notes and managing time. Ms. Castillo's students are learning positive peer learning behaviors, and they have been provided with many, many opportunities to respond. Interviewing is one way to get to know each other and build community.

SUPPORT LEARNING APPROPRIATE BEHAVIOR THROUGH KIND WORDS

Teachers can also support children at risk for social behavior problems through community building. One strategy that has been recommended and researched is *peer tootling,* which is a version of positive peer reporting (Skinner, Cashwell, & Skinner, 2000). When using peer tootling, teachers have children catch each other being good and then report on this positive behavior. Thus this is the opposite of tattling. Teachers could have students report during specific times on what others have done as part of class meetings, or they can target a specific skill or student they want to see the focus of positive peer reporting. Examples of each are presented next. A planning form is presented in Figure 2.2.

Tootling to Support Molly. Molly's second-grade teacher, Ms. Miller, really wants other children to notice that Molly does display a lot of good behavior rather than focusing only on her problem behavior. So Ms. Miller tells Molly she is going to have her classmates report to her when they see her being kind to others. They go over the following ways she could be kind:

★ Using kind words with friends and adults, such as *please* and *thank you*
★ Helping another person by holding a door, carrying something, or warning that person of something
★ Letting someone else go first
★ Sharing materials
★ Letting someone else do something she wanted to do

Then Ms. Miller goes over the same examples with her class and instructs them to look for such behaviors and write them on a note card to be placed in a tootle box to be drawn from at the end of the day. To make children more interested in participating, Ms. Miller gives the student whose card was chosen a small treat from their class prize box (a Jolly Rancher candy, pencil, sticker, etc.). Molly is so proud when her peers recognize something she has done that is positive. Molly's parents also approved and enjoyed the notes they received communicating the positive peer comments.

Group Example: Tootle Time—Be Kind. If Ms. Miller were going to use the strategy with the whole class, she would still provide instruction on examples and the procedures for positive peer reporting. Then she could choose from several different options, including the following:

★ Having the students report every day at the end of a class one thing they noticed someone else did that was kind that day
★ Using a "positive peer box" or a "tootle jar" and reviewing at the end of the day a few examples from the box, similar to the Molly example
★ Having peers share with each other and then sign a form that someone caught them being kind
★ Including a tootle poster board in class where children can write what they observed and by whom on a sticky note and post it on the board

Variations of this strategy are common and include, for example, developing an "I caught you box" where students catch each other

Figure 2.2 Tootle Time

Determine who (individual or group)	
Determine behavior	
Explicitly teach process	
Determine tootle time	
Select rewards—for children who participate in tootles and the target recipients of the tootles (whole class or individual)	Participation: Recipient:

being good, write a comment on a note card, and place it in the box (Mitschelen, 2013).

"Good Deeds Tree" (Jones & Jones, 2001, p. 143). Similar to tootling, the good deeds tree supports the need to help one another. Accordingly, a large paper branch or tree is displayed on the bulletin board or wall. Students are then encouraged to notice when other students are doing something nice or helpful, write it on a leaf made of construction paper, and then place it on the tree. Children who can't write well could ask a peer for assistance, or for very young children, they could report to adults who then write the deed for them.

Two-Slip Game. The teacher cuts two strips of paper for each student in class and then passes each student two pieces of paper. Students write their names on the top of each piece of paper and then return them to the teacher. The teacher then has all students draw two pieces of paper from two different students; they do not keep their own paper if they draw it. Then the students are instructed to anonymously write a positive comment about the students they drew. The teacher then collects, sorts, and hands them back to the students. According to Mitschelen (2013), "This activity really does work and is a classroom favorite. Kids will often use their slips of paper as bookmarks to remind them of positive things others felt about them" (p. 1).

Comment Fan (Mitschelen, 2013). Similar to the activity described above, teachers can also have students fold a piece of paper into a certain number of equal parts (four or six). Then students write their name on the top and pass either to the left or the right. Students receiving the fan write a positive comment about the person on part of the fan and then pass it on to the next person. This activity can be timed to make the pace faster or to make it seem more like a game as well. The papers (also known as accordion comment fans) are returned to the student.

The first author's college students did this activity when presenting different community-building activities. She liked her fan comments so much that she put them on her refrigerator for a week! Alternatively, the students could take their fans home, a quick and meaningful way to share positive feedback with families.

SUMMARY

There are a multitude of community-building activities teachers can use for students of all ages and with professional colleagues. The main thing to stress is how important it is to use them often, especially during the beginning of the year, after breaks, and when class community seems low. Community building is very important for children who are struggling and need to take risks to learn in a supportive environment.

3 Using Data-Based Decision Making

Mrs. Smith collects information on how many spelling words Laura has completed correctly this week. Then she enters the information on a graph and shows Laura her progress over the last four weeks. Laura has met her goal (80% accuracy), and they celebrate with a high five. They set a new goal of 100%.

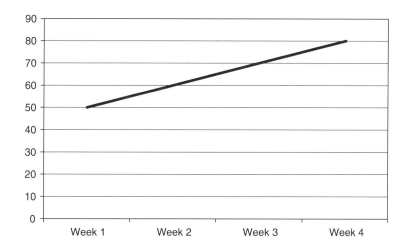

✦

Mrs. Smith collects information on how many words David spelled correctly this week and graphs this information as well. He didn't make any progress from last week. Mrs. Smith and David make a plan for increasing his practice for the next week. They write it down and both sign the plan. Then Mrs. Smith sends the information home to David's parents with a gentle reminder to help him practice at home.

◆

Juan is struggling to learn his multiplication facts. Mr. Miller and Juan make a plan to collect information on how many facts he knows correctly every day, and they target specific facts. Once they break down the facts, they practice every day for 10 minutes, and Juan quickly learns most of his facts. The bar graphs displaying what he needs to work on are helpful for both Juan and Mr. Miller.

◆

Mrs. Chin develops a chart to monitor how often children in her classroom are sent to the safe spot and how often they are sent to the office (i.e., office disciplinary referral). She uses this information to determine which children may need more support in her classroom. She consults with the school psychologist to help determine what interventions she could use to support each child.

This chapter includes a discussion of why data are very important for supporting children and teachers in classroom settings. Information on the types of data that can be used for decision making is also included. Multiple examples are provided.

DATA AND ASSESSMENT DEFINED

Data used in educational settings include the multiple sources of information teachers gather to inform teaching and planning (Brawley & Stormont, in press; Copple & Bredekamp, 2009). Data are gathered through the process of assessment, which includes determining children's progress through multiple methods, including, but not limited to, reviewing children's work, having conversations or interviews with children to determine how they are solving problems and if they have developed misconceptions, administering individual criterion or norm-referenced assessments, conducting direct observation, and talking to children's families (Copple & Bredekamp, 2009).

What Data Should Teachers Collect?

Teachers gather multiple sources of data on children every day. The important thing to remember for general educators who work with children at risk for failure is that data need to be gathered more systematically and analyzed more frequently to determine if children are responding to teaching methods or if they need more support. Teachers need to consider what data they already collect and how to supplement this with additional sources if needed.

How Can Teachers Use Data More Systematically?

The examples at the beginning of this chapter highlight simple ways teachers can use academic and social behavior data to determine children's progress. Figure 3.1 includes an interview with a third-grade teacher regarding how she uses data and the importance of closely monitoring children who are at risk for failure.

Figure 3.1   Teacher Feature

Ms. Mathes, a Third-Grade Teacher, Describes Her Thoughts on Data Collection and Use

How do you use data to monitor children's progress? I use computer data such as STAR Reading [http://www.renlearn.com/sr/]. I use DRA2 [http://www.mypearsontraining.com/products/dra2/tutorials.asp]. I use fact tests (especially multiplication). I use spelling tests three times a year. I use student writing samples. I feel it's important to look at more than one piece of data. I would not rely solely on the STAR program. I like the one-on-one of the DRA2, but the STAR lets me know more how students will perform independently. You also have to know your students by using anecdotal data. Maybe they perform great on the DRA2 because that is one-on-one with the teacher. However, when they read independently, they are off task and don't stick with one book. That will affect the type of book I put them in. The DRA2 might indicate that they are a Level 34, but I would put them in a shorter book, maybe even easier to help them stay on task. You can't rely solely on a number without taking behaviors into account.

When data indicate a child is not on target, what do you do? I use multiple data sources and my observations to decide on the area I think they need the most help with. They may need help with 10 different reading skills, but you can't improve them all at once. I pick one that I think will have the most impact and work on that with the student. I may also have a tutor of some sort work with that student on that skill also. When that skill is consistently improving or mastered (shown through data), I would work on a new skill. I would also be sure parents knew what skill we were working on so they could support it at home.

Teacher Friendly Data Sources

Teachers are some of the busiest people we know, and collecting data takes time. It is also a skill set, and most teachers report that they have not received enough preservice training or professional development to help them feel comfortable with collecting data. Yet for children at risk, in order to meet social and academic goals, more systematic, frequent, and even sophisticated data collection is called for. In previous examples in this chapter, typical kinds of school data have been recommended, including reading inventories, student work samples, and graphing progress using either number correct or percentage scores for spelling or math tests that often occur at weekly intervals. In Chapter 8, recommendations will be made for consultation and collaborative support with school specialist personnel, such as the school psychologist, who can support teachers in collecting reliable and valid data to inform instruction and intervention. Following are descriptions of two more efficient and easy-to-use methods for data collection that teachers can use themselves.

Frequency counts (Alberto & Troutman, 2011) and *scatterplots* are teacher friendly methods for collecting data, especially data on behavior (Thomas, 2007). To gather data using a frequency count, the teacher first identifies a behavior of concern, generally one that has not responded to his or her typical behavior management strategies. For a child at risk, common chronic behaviors include talking out or being out of one's seat. In these cases, the teacher can just count how many times this happens during a certain time period, for example, during reading class or before lunch. Easy ways to count include making tallies on paper, using a golf clicker, or even moving pennies from one pocket to another while teaching. Each day, the data can be graphed. Once the teacher has recorded three to 10 days, a clear picture should emerge of how often the student is really calling out or out of his or her seat. At this point, the teacher can begin new strategies for change. For example, if Sarah, a second grader, typically is out of her seat five or more times during a single class period, her teacher can set an initial goal for Sarah to be out of her seat just three times. Showing Sarah the data is often helpful, and many children are motivated by seeing the results of their efforts to improve on the graph. Sarah's teacher can support change using this strategy: She gives Sarah three green cards to keep at her desk during each subject. Each time Sarah is out of her seat, the teacher collects one green card. This physical prompt can help Sarah become more aware of, and therefore learn to manage, her own behavior. And her teacher should continue to take data; once Sarah is successfully meeting the goal of just three times out of her seat, it can be further reduced to a goal of two, then one. Sarah's teacher gives Sarah lots of positive feedback for meeting her goals and may even provide Sarah with a favorite tangible reward such as a sticker or extra time with a friend.

A second simple way for teachers to collect data is through use of a scatterplot. In earlier examples, Ms. Mathes mentioned that she used multiple data sources. A scatterplot is a good one to include when a teacher is not sure when or why the problem behavior is occurring. It is a great way to clear up any misconceptions about the problem because scatterplots provide a clear picture! A scatterplot is a grid organized by day and broken into time periods. In the example that follows, Sarah's teacher is unsure of when and why the problem behavior is occurring. In this case, it seems to the teacher that Sarah is calling out every few minutes! This behavior is interrupting instruction in her classroom. Sarah's comments are off topic and funny; other students in the class are laughing and going off task too. Some students have even started to call out themselves. As Sarah's behavior increased, Sarah's teacher could not keep up using a frequency count or other strategies she knew. She is very concerned about the impact Sarah's behavior is having on instruction and everyone's learning. While the teacher has invited the school psychologist (see Chapter 8) to come and observe, she would like to have some data to show at the upcoming meeting next week. She decides to use a scatterplot. In the example that follows, Sarah's teacher collected data for five days. She took data during every period before lunch, and she divided each period into approximately 15-minute increments, leaving time for the beginning of the school day and transitions between periods. Sarah's teacher uses Time Timer (a visual timer that uses the color red on a clock to show available time; http://www.timetimer.com) so she can see the elapsed time easily. On the scatterplot, all she does is put an X during any time increments in which the behavior occurred. It does not matter how many times or how intense the behavior is, just if it happened. Sometimes, if a teacher wants to record frequency or intensity, he or she can use a code instead of an X; for example, an X means a lot of behavior, a / means some behavior, and an empty box means that the target behavior did not occur. In Sarah's case, by Day 3 of data collection, her teacher was starting to understand the reasons for the problem behavior better. She decided she also wanted to talk to the school psychologist about some further testing for reading. Nearly all of Sarah's calling out during reading class was happening during silent reading time or around the time when Sarah might be called on to read aloud in class. When Sarah's teacher looked over her lesson plans, she realized that Sarah's "bad" day in math was the day they had worked on word problem solving, and similarly in science, during small-group, activity-based instruction, Sarah was not calling out—only when reading the science textbook and even when reading directions prior to beginning activities. Scatterplots are good visual representations of patterns in behavior, and when combined with other data sources, they can help to plan effective interventions.

Subject	Time	Day 1	Day 2	Day 3	Day 4	Day 5
Reading	8:15	X		X	X	X
	8:30	X	X	X	X	X
	8:45	X	X		X	X
Math	9:05		X			
	9:20		X			
	9:35		X			
Science	9:55	X		X	X	X
	10:10	X	X			
	10:25	X				
Art	10:45					
	11:00					
	11:15					

An Interview With Third-Grade Teacher, Ms. Mathes

Why do you think general educators need to collect data to monitor progress especially for children at risk? I think using data can be a valuable teaching tool. I do think you need to be cautious in using it though. I think you need to be sure that you are collecting data for a child-centered reason, not just to make a pretty chart or to give to administration. I think you need to be sure you know the difference between collecting data and teaching. Things like the STAR online reading test and multiplication fact tests aren't interventions. They don't teach kids how to read or multiply. They are ways to check progress. I think collecting data is a way to see if how you are teaching is having an effect on students. It's also a way for students to see the results of their hard work concretely and get them motivated. If you are using a strategy and you see no improvement in the data, you are wasting valuable time that an at-risk student doesn't have. You do need to take into account classroom observation as data too. Maybe the data are not improving on a computerized test, but you are seeing more enthusiasm for reading and more on-task reading behavior for that student. Some things are harder to see in "data" form but are still important.

Teachers could use the following points to direct data collection:

★ What data do I already collect to monitor progress (e.g., weekly spelling tests, weekly math facts, writing work)?

★ How can I establish a systematic way to use this data? This can include entering data into a data system or making handmade graphs.

★ How can I analyze data? It is important to have trend lines on graphs based on where children should be in terms of progress. This information can be made based on guidelines from publishers, curriculum standards, and so on. Teachers can also monitor growth on specific skills or behavior goals by simply checking mastery of different targets over time.

★ What technology resources are available to help collect and analyze data? There are many technology resources available to support teachers in helping children at risk.

A great website for teacher tools and support in planning data collection and analysis is Intervention Central (http://www .interventioncentral.org). On this website, the multiple types of data teachers can collect are discussed, including global skills checklists, frequency counts for problem behavior, daily behavior cards, mastery logs, and curriculum-based measurement. There are sample forms and templates teachers can use to make their own tools targeted specifically for their students' needs. Furthermore, there is a wonderful resource on understanding how to use the data teachers collect in a systematic manner (Wright, 2010).

Figure 3.2 includes a nice example of how one third-grade teacher, Ms. Mathes, displayed data for four academic skills. The graph template was created by Michele Schlottach, who is also a third-grade teacher. This graph was used in a parent-teacher conference to explain Taylor's progress to her parents. This was the first conference, so the September/October targets were highlighted. The graphs displayed trend lines for average growth of third graders across the school year. The hand-drawn points represented data Ms. Mathes had collected on Taylor. As can be seen, Taylor was right on target for three of the four skills. Ms. Mathes and Taylor's parents discussed that she needed more practice on her addition and subtraction facts and developed a plan to work on these skills. At the next conference, the same graph was used, and Taylor's progress exceeded expectations.

Teachers can also determine main ideas for lesson plans and have all students in class complete "exit slips" with key lesson points in order to determine if they have learned the content (National Council of Teachers of English [NCTE], 2013). These slips can then be collected, and teachers can determine if students learned the main ideas and/or if some students need different levels of support. The use of this informal assessment is simple! These slips can also be used for review and could be posted to show students' interests (NCTE, 2013). According to the NCTE (2013), steps for using this practice are as follows:

★ Determine what concept the exit slip should include for you to gather data on progress.
  ★ On the Reading Rockets website (http://www.readingrockets .org) some good examples of prompts for exit slips include the following:
    ☆ "Write one question you have about today's lesson."
    ☆ "Explain why Canada is not considered a melting pot."
    ☆ "Write three words with the long *o* sound."
    ☆ "Of the three graphs we studied today, which one did you find most useful? Why?"
  ★ At the end of the lesson, pass out the exit slips and ask students to complete them.
★ Typically, the exit slip will include a prompt related to the lesson and what students' learned; the prompt can be presented orally, posted somewhere visually, or each student can be given an exit slip with the prompt on it. There should be a place for students to insert their names, unless teachers want to collect some data and allow for confidentiality (although this is difficult because teachers often recognize their students' handwriting).

Figure 3.2

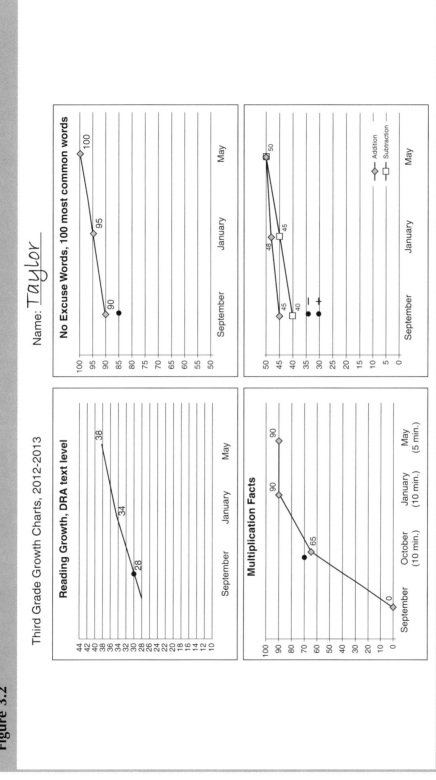

Third Grade Growth Charts, 2012-2013

Name: Taylor

★ Provide paper for students if the prompt is posted or stated orally; this then becomes the exit slip.
★ Collect exit slips and review for determining if you need to reteach, if you need to differentiate instruction for some students, or if students mastered the information.
★ Exit slips can be published and/or included in an assessment portfolio to document growth or mastery of certain concepts.

There are numerous resources on the Internet on exit slips, sample templates, ways to use them, and technology supports. A few websites that have many resources for children at risk are listed next, along with web addresses to their materials on exit slips:

★ readwritethink, a website supported by the International Reading Association, the National Council of English Teachers, and Verizon's Thinkfinity provides educators and families with access to high-quality instructional materials for language arts (http://www .readwritethink.org/professional-development/strategy-guides/ exit-slips-30760.html).
★ Reading rockets, a service of WETA, Washington's major public broadcasting channel and largely funded by the U.S. Department of Education, Office of Special Education Programs, offers research-based strategies to help teachers and families support reading development (http://www.readingrockets.org/strategies/ exit_slips).
★ Edudemic is an education technology news site with a goal of connecting educators to technology (http://edudemic .com/2012/12/12-digital-tools-to-implement-exit-slips).

Use Data to Set and Monitor Goals

Data are also very useful for setting and monitoring goals. Children can help set goals for improvement. If children are working on increasing their speed on something, such as reading decoding or math facts, they can set goals to increase their time. Figure 3.3 is an example of how the simple insertion of the time at the top of a math fact sheet was used to monitor Taylor's progress in increasing her speed. The comments from the teacher "WOW! 2 minutes faster" and the comment from the student who wrote "Thanks" show that they are both engaged in monitoring progress.

Figure 3.4 is an example of how these data are inserted into students' journals so they can monitor their progress and keep track of their accuracy and fluency (times). Figure 3.5 is a blank form that can be reproduced and used across all math facts and could be easily adapted to monitor and set goals—for example, for spelling words, reading decoding,

Figure 3.3

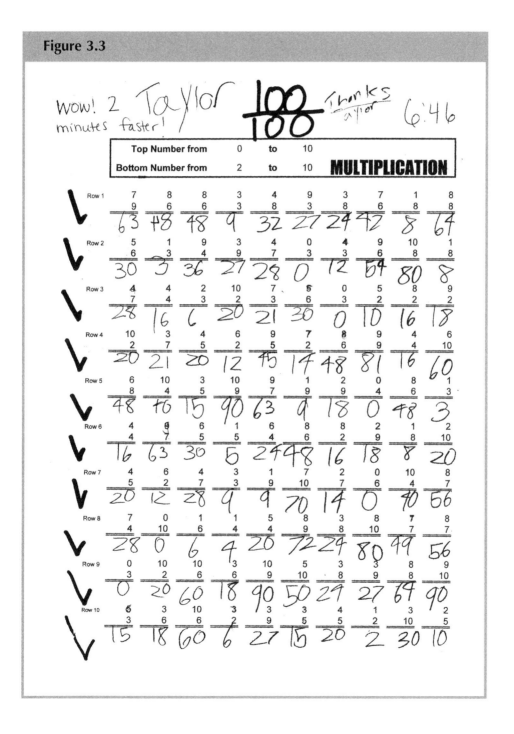

Figure 3.4

Name _Taylor_

My Multiplication Test Record

Date	Number Correct	I did	Time	I did ....
11/1/12	70	~~Better, Same, Worse~~	10.00	~~Better, Same, Worse~~
11/28/12	89	(Better,) Same, Worse	10:00	Better, (Same) Worse
12/6/12	100	(Better,) Same, Worse	9:45	(Better) Same, Worse
12/12/12	100	Better, Same, Worse	8:46	Better, Same, Worse
12/19/12	100	Better, Same, Worse	6:46	Better, Same, Worse
13/9/1	100	Better, Same, Worse	5:22	Better, Same, Worse
13/2/6	100	(Better,) Same, Worse	5:55	(Better) Same, Worse
13/13/1	100	(Better,) Same, Worse	6:15	Better, (Same, Worse)
13/16/1	100	Better, Same, Worse	8:19	Better, Same, Worse
13/23/1	100	Better, Same, Worse	6:42	Better, Same, Worse
13/30/1	100	Better, Same, Worse	8:08	Better, Same, Worse
	100	Better, (Same, Worse)	5:52	(Better,) Same, Worse
		Better, Same, Worse		Better, Same, Worse
		Better, Same, Worse		Better, Same, Worse
		Better, Same, Worse		Better, Same, Worse
		Better, Same, Worse		Better, Same, Worse

reading comprehension, or improving specific skills in written expression. These data can be reviewed with the information from the journal in Figure 3.4 to monitor progress and set additional goals. Figure 3.6 is a planning form teachers can use to target specific skills or areas they want to monitor.

Figure 3.5   Blank Planning Sheet for Practice and Goals

I know these facts well: _____

_____

_____

_____

_____

I need to practice these facts: _____

_____

_____

_____

_____

My goal for next week's test is to (choose one):

☐ Make a score of _____

☐ Get a time of _____

This is what I plan to do to reach my goal:

★   This is how I will practice: _____

★   I will practice these days: _____

★   I will practice this long each day: _____

Figure 3.6 Progress Monitoring Sheet

Student: _____

Area/Skills Targeted: _____

	Area/Skill 1	Area/Skill 2	Area/Skill 3
Date/progress[a]			
Date/progress			
Date/progress			
Date/progress			
Date/progress			

a. Progress can be tracked according to yes/no for a specific skill, a brief summary of performance (e.g., correctly answered four of five comprehension questions), or percentage of accuracy.

HOW CAN TEACHERS USE TECHNOLOGY TO COLLECT DATA?

There are so many ways teachers can use technology to guide all aspects of planning, instruction, and progress monitoring that we devote an entire chapter to using technology to support children at risk (see Chapter 7). Following are a few options that would be helpful for data management. Time Timer (http://www.timetimer.com) is an application (app) available for handhelds, tablets, and computers. Teachers can use this visual timer to improve academic and social behavior. It is useful to teach time concepts, monitor classroom transitions, keep time for testing, gather data on behavior, and help students focus on tasks within allotted time. Kid Coach: The KidTools Support System (http://kidtools.org) includes four support programs to help children at risk be successful: (a) KidTools (Miller, Fitzgerald, Koury, Mitchem, & Hollingsead, 2007), (b) KidSkills, (c) Picture Tools, and (d) Teacher Tools. This website provides eKidTools and eKidSkills for elementary children and iKidTools and iKidSkills for older students. The content of this website includes strategies for behavior management, problem solving, organization, and planning. Additionally, these programs focus on helping teachers support students in learning to self-manage, a critical goal for school success and quality of life. Another app for data management is Percentally (http://ericsailers.com/percentally.html). It can be used for tallies and can convert tallies into percentages to reflect accuracy in the academic or social behavior. One more useful tool is Behavior Tracker Pro (http://www.behaviortrackerpro.com). This app helps teachers easily and quickly collect and graph data to see student progress in behavior and skills. Many more tools exist, and once teachers become familiar with a few apps, they can search the web to find options that are more current or that may better meet their needs.

COLLABORATE WHEN MORE DATA ARE NEEDED

It is important for educators to understand when more data are needed to understand students' needs for support. Chapter 8 directs teachers to various professionals who can be consulted to assist in collecting and analyzing data.

SUMMARY

This chapter provided teachers with simple ways to use data they already collect as well as ways to be more strategic about collecting data to inform intervention needs. Examples were presented that illustrated how data can be used for goal setting and progress monitoring. Especially for students at risk for failure, it is vital that teachers consistently monitor progress, communicate data-based decisions with families, and reach out to other professionals when they need support.

4 Increase Time to Practice With Feedback

Children who are at risk often need more time to practice skills (Burns, Griffiths, Parson, Tilly, & VanDerHayden, 2007; Stormont, Lewis, Beckner, & Johnson, 2008; Stormont, Reinke, Herman, & Lembke, 2012). We can foster resilience by building children's skills so their likelihood for failure decreases. It is important to remember that children may need to practice specific academic skills and social skills. The need for practice to occur *with feedback* is critical. Children can practice by themselves, but without observation and feedback, they could be practicing the wrong answer or performing a skill or behavior incorrectly. When children practice using the wrong answer, it is much more difficult for them to learn the right answer. It is also a tremendous misuse of time.

The *first* step to incorporating more practice with feedback opportunities for children is to *use data to figure out who and what needs more practice* (Burns et al., 2007). As we discussed in the former chapter, data can highlight who needs practice with various academic skills such as spelling words; reading decoding; reading comprehension; math facts; vocabulary knowledge; written expression; specific social studies topics, such as presidents, states, and capitals; and so on. Data can also help determine who needs more social skills practice, such as understanding feelings, using words to talk through problems, and strategies for dealing with frustrating situations. These data can also help determine skills the entire class needs to practice more, skills small groups of children need to practice, and individual children's needs.

Next, set a goal for how much time you think specific children will need. For example, one child who is at risk may really be struggling with only basic fact knowledge, such as spelling words and math facts, whereas another child may be struggling with everything in the curriculum at that time. The entire class may need to practice math facts more. Small groups of children may need to read more to build fluency.

Third, find opportunities for more practice that don't include taking away recess. Children who need extra practice should not spend time waiting in lines if that down time can be used for instruction. Opportunities often present in elementary schools for 15 minutes of practice time include the following:

★ Waiting on the bus in the morning
★ Waiting in the cafeteria or gymnasium in the morning for teachers to come get class
★ Waiting in the hallway for class to begin
★ Waiting in the hallway to go to lunch
★ Packing up and transitioning to bus, parent pick up at end of the day

Other opportunities for practice that don't include recess are times when children are eating, *if* they would rather eat somewhere else with an adult and then spend time working. You can also identify other times where children are working independently on projects or activities (e.g., writing in journals) where specific children would benefit from having someone work with them on specific skills. For example, if the class is working on something that a child does not have the prerequisite skills for, then working on those skills would be a better use of time. If a child can't read at the required level and doesn't have required math skills, then that child cannot be successful independently working on the assigned math. He will just sit there feeling lost. He knows he can't do it. Time would be better spent building skills to help catch him up to grade level. Given that often many children need skill building in specific areas, small groups of children can be pulled for increased practice time. Furthermore, in some cases, entire classes may be behind in specific areas, and it would be beneficial to use some of the opportunities to practice with the entire class.

Fourth, find people to help provide practice opportunities. Professionals available in most elementary settings who could assist in supporting children through increased practice with feedback include the following:

★ School psychologists
★ School counselors
★ School nurse
★ Administrators
★ Preservice teachers
★ Parent volunteers

★ Office staff
★ Cross-age tutors (older students tutoring younger students)
★ Peers

Outline the practice plan and go over the plan with the assisting professional and the child. Have the plan in a folder, freezer bag, small box, or something similar to hand to the person. It is very important to develop materials to support structured and efficient use of time during practice. It is also important to go over the plan and what the practice opportunities should look like. If the professional does not have extensive teaching or clinical experience, schedule the first session to occur somewhere you can observe him or her and provide feedback (e.g., in the hall outside your classroom).

Make the practice fun! Make sure people working with the child understand the importance of building some rapport and providing encouragement for working hard. Use of small reinforcers for effort is also a motivator for many students. It is important to use rewards often if children perceive working on basic skills (math facts, spelling) as challenging and boring. Tangible rewards and positive praise are often needed for children to increase and sustain effort.

Provide supports and list the target supports in the plan. As the child's teacher you will know more about his or her needs than the assisting professional. Accordingly, it is important to include these needs for support on the plan. We will address these more in Chapters 5 and 6. Examples are provided in the sample plans at the end of this chapter.

Technology-based skills practice. There are many options for skills practice using technology. Furthermore, many of these options are highly engaging, include built in reinforcement, and may even be in game formats. Children can practice independently or with a peer. Examples include flashcards that can function on a variety of devices; are ready-made; can be created, synced, shared, and include data collection options; and have special features such as sounds, images, and text to speech (http://www.flashcardapps.info/filter/srs-plus/). Math applications include virtual manipulatives (see National Library of Virtual Manipulatives at http://nlvm.usu.edu/en/nav/vlibrary.html) and skill practice games. For example, Math Facts Pro (http://www.techforteachers.net/apps---math-practice.html) has information for students and teachers; is leveled by operation, grade level, and skill level within grade level; and collects data. Reading and language options exist too. Starfall (http://www.starfall.com) provides opportunities to practice each of the "big five" reading components of early reading (phonemic awareness, phonics, fluency, vocabulary, comprehension) recommended by the National Reading Panel (National Institute of Child Health and Human

Development, 2000), and ArtikPix (http://ericsailers.com/artikpix.html), a language application, allows children to self-monitor their own speech production using voice and video recording, along with recorded audio as models. ArtikPix is compatible with iPhone, iPad, and iTouch, includes flashcards and matching activities for sound practice, and has built-in scoring options for data.

Recently, the second author observed Mr. Patton during a middle school vocabulary lesson. Mr. Patton has developed a high-quality and intensive vocabulary curriculum to complement and augment the district curriculum. Many of his students would be considered at risk, have performed poorly on district and national assessments in reading, and need extra vocabulary practice. During this observation, Mr. Patton engaged his students by inviting them to play a game called Free Rice (http://freerice.com/#/english-vocabulary/1447). Free Rice was developed by the United Nations World Food Program and has a social justice mission. To play this game, students click on the correct definition/reasonable synonym for the target word. For each correct answer, the site donates 10 grains of rice to their hunger relief program, paid for by site advertisers. This engaging game branches so that a correct answer is followed by a harder question and an incorrect answer is followed by an easier question. Furthermore, students can be guided to content vocabulary grouped by subject. It is possible to create or join a group to play and compete. Total scores and rankings are accessible. In Mr. Patton's class, the digital divide was evident. The computer cart included computers that did not work at all, did not have power cords, and had missing keys on the keyboard. Yet he and his students persisted because of the game. Incentives were provided to students who reached higher levels. Technology can be an effective medium for sustaining attention and helping students persist in challenging (and sometimes, boring) yet needed practice. In this case, Mr. Patton's students spent an intensive hour practicing high-level vocabulary. Although Mr. Patton's students were in middle school this website is also very appropriate for upper elementary and includes a variety of subject areas.

Increase opportunities for practice at home by developing specific support materials, knowing who is available in families to provide support, and setting reasonable goals and time with families. Finding ways to practice skills that fit families' busy schedules is also important. At the end of this chapter, there is a handout that could be sent home with specific directions for how this could be supported. Families need to understand why five-minute practice sessions are important and then need specific instructions on where and when they could use the activities. Using down time that isn't very interesting is a good time for these activities. Examples include waiting at the doctor's office, waiting at the bus stop, or while riding on public transportation; also, a sibling or family member who isn't driving could use the time to practice in a vehicle.

Monitor progress with the same data collected to target children's needs. Children who are at risk for failure need to be in educational intensive care. This means they need to be monitored closely until they catch up with same-age peers. Just as a doctor monitors patients' vital signs, educators need to monitor children's vital signs in terms of their educational progress.

QUICK ONE-MINUTE PRACTICE SESSIONS: PREVIEWS INSTEAD OF REVIEWS

Children at risk need frequent reminders of the rules and routines of the classroom. You will know which children need the opportunity to practice and what they need to practice based on errors that are made. For example, if a student always runs to the door when it is time for recess or lunch, he or she would benefit from this type of support. A quick review of these expectations followed by a quick practice session can help get children ready for success. There are times, especially at the beginning of the year, when the entire class would benefit from previews.

Some examples of when this would be useful include the following:

★ A student talks out of turn during large group.
★ A student plays with other students' lockers while lined up and waiting to go to lunch.
★ A student refuses to leave a game of Four Square after he is out.
★ A student yells for help during independent seat work.
★ A student talks instead of eating during lunch and is hungry the rest of the day.
★ A student forgets what she is supposed to be doing during journal time.
★ A student says "You're stupid" and other unkind things when working with others in groups.
★ The entire class is getting in trouble for talking in the hall.

A quick practice session would get the student ready for what he or she needs to be doing instead of what the student is currently doing. This process is also called precorrection, which refers to using past mistakes to correct a potential future problem before it has a chance to occur (Stormont & Reinke, 2008; Stormont et al., 2008). This strategy works well with additional supports such as praise and visual supports, which are discussed in Chapters 5 and 6. Essentially, teachers can use the following prompts to determine who and what needs practice. A blank form with these prompts is included at the end of the chapter.

Who?	What needs practice?

Jackson	**Lining up to go to recess**
	Quick practice session
	    Put away materials
	    Push chair in
	    Walk quietly to the door

Sandra	**Using kind words when working with peers** Review kind words and unkind words Review what to say if you disagree with someone's idea (e.g., "Let's keep thinking about this") Review what to say to encourage others (e.g., "Nice idea") Review what to do if frustrated (e.g., have the teacher come and coach)

David	**Knowing what to do when he needs help with work**
	Review process for getting assistance
	    Raise his hand
	    Raise flag at desk indicating help is needed
	    Ask a specific agreed-upon peer
	    Walk to teacher's desk if the teacher is not working with someone

SUMMARY OF KEY POINTS

In this chapter, the following key points were discussed:

★ The importance of practice for children who are behind
★ How to plan and find opportunities to support more practice
★ How to locate people to support more practice
★ The importance of data for targeting specific goals, assessing students' current performance in an area, and monitoring progress over time
★ How to get ahead of problems by conducting quick previews to avoid problems

Figure 4.1 Sample Practice Plan: De Quan's Plan

Goal: De Quan will increase his accuracy and speed on target math facts to 25 completed in 3 minutes.

Current performance (baseline): De Quan accurately answers 10 of the 25 facts in 10 minutes.

Needs for support:
★ Manipulatives and number lines to build number sense
★ Needs to stand while practicing

Motivators:
★ Positive attention (You are working hard!)
★ Sticker for effort halfway through practice
★ Jolly Rancher candy at the end

Data collection schedule: Once a week, record accuracy and time required to complete 25 words.

Date:	Number Correct:	Time:
10–1	11	9 minutes
10–8	15	8 minutes
10–15	16	7 min, 30 sec
_____	_____	_____
_____	_____	_____

(Continued)

Figure 4.1 (Continued)

Professional Assisting With Plan	Plan Materials	Times	Where
Molly, school psychologist	Freezer bag with 25 flashcards, small counters, number line to 20, extra paper, and a small number of stickers and Jolly Rancher candies	M, W, F 15 minutes at beginning of day during wait and transition times	Molly's office

Figure 4.2 Practice Plan

_____ Plan

Goal: _____

_____

_____

Current performance (baseline): _____

_____

_____

Needs for support:

Motivators:

Data collection schedule: _____

Date: Progress:

_____

_____

_____

_____

(Continued)

Figure 4.2 (Continued)

_____ Plan

Professional Assisting With Plan	Plan Materials	Times	Where

Figure 4.3 A Family Guide to Five-Minute Activities

Support Your Child's Success in School With Five-Minute Activities

(See the steps on the back to get started.)

Why? No time is too little where practice is concerned. Even five minutes here and there makes a big difference and adds up when done often

(Continued)

Figure 4.3 (Continued)

STEPS

1. Set a goal with your child's teacher: Example: Goal is to find _____ times a week your family can use a 5-minute activity with your child.

2. Plan possible times/places: For example, in the car, waiting for the bus, before school, right after school, in the doctor's office. Times/places: _____

   _____

   _____

3. Work with teacher to plan for what to work on and keep the plans with you. Types of skills may include math facts, spelling words, state capitals. Skills:

   _____

4. Keep track of time; make it a game by saying, "It is 5-minute activity time."

5. "Remember when you are done, you will get a little reward."

6. Say, "Ready . . . Set . . . GO!

7. If your child is working hard and sticking with it—at 1, 2, 3, and 4 minutes say, "You are working hard!"

8. Have a sticker or small treat ready when done if your child worked hard for 5 minutes. Reward effort during these activities not correctness.

9. Keep track of how your child is doing; once he or she reaches the teacher-set goal (e.g., spell all target words correctly), have another 5-minute activity ready.

Figure 4.4

Preview Prompt Sheet

Who?	What needs practice?
_____	_____ Quick practice session: _____ _____ _____ _____

5 Teach and Support Desired Social Behavior

It is clear that teachers need to be prepared to support children's use of appropriate social behavior in schools. As discussed in the first chapter, the percentage of children who will display problem behavior is high and the need to support their development of more adaptive behavior is critical. However, often teachers and schools are not prepared to support social behavior. In recent research that surveyed general and special educators, the following findings were noted (Reinke, Stormont, Herman, Puri, & Goel, 2011; Stormont, Reinke, & Herman, 2011a):

★ Most teachers reported they wanted more support for managing behavior problems in their classrooms.
★ General educators were more likely than special educators to report that practices that are *not* evidence-based are evidence based.
★ Special educators were more likely than general educators to report practices that *are* evidence-based as evidence based.

The greater the number of risk factors children experience, the greater the likelihood that children will need support (Stormont et al., 2012). Children who are at risk are in the general education setting, and general educators need to be prepared to teach social skills. It is clear that many children who are at risk receive little, no, or negative examples of appropriate social skills prior to school entry. Other children who are at risk who do receive support prior to school entry still need more support because of their own characteristics even when their environments are rich with opportunities. Thus, we cannot assume a child understands what educators mean when we request competencies such as being "respectful" and using "kind words." Either because of their within-child characteristics or environmental influences or both, many children need to be supported in learning school behavior expectations (Stormont et al., 2008; Sugai, 2011). As discussed in Chapter 1, when children enter school and are met with expectations to demonstrate skills that they do not have or do not know when to use, the school environment magnifies a child's risk for failure in school. Increasingly, schools across the country are implementing systems of positive behavior support (schoolwide positive behavioral interventions and supports, or SW-PBIS) to support appropriate behavior and increase academic success for all children. Within systems of SW-PBIS, in theory, all children have a leveled playing field because there is not an assumption that children come to school with specific social skills and, accordingly, all children receive direct instruction and support for demonstrating social skills (Stormont et al., 2008; Sugai, 2011).

Prevention-based systems allow for the intensity of the intervention children need to be based on their response to increasingly greater supports. SW-PBIS includes a continuum of supports. If the Tier 1 interventions are implemented with consistency and the way they were intended, then 80% of children will respond to these supports and not need any other intervention. The next level of support is a secondary level, called Tier 2 supports, and approximately 10% to 15% of children need this level of support as they were not successful with only the universal supports. The final tier, Tier 3, includes children who need more intensive and often highly individualized supports.

Some target universal and secondary-level supports that are often used within systems of SW-PBIS and that could be easily used by general educators are presented in this chapter. Overall, this chapter includes information on simple and extremely effective strategies to support appropriate behavior. Specific strategies that will be discussed include explicit teaching, precorrection, active supervision, positive reinforcement strategies, and understanding setting factors that support problem behavior, including the function of behavior. Additional strategies for specific types of behavior problems, including escape-maintained behavior (behavior children display to get out of a task or activity) and mood monitoring will be provided. Finally, at the end of the chapter we point out that after simple strategies are tried, teachers need to understand that professionals are available who have expertise in schools to assist with more extensive supports.

EXPLICIT TEACHING AND SUPPORTING APPROPRIATE BEHAVIOR

Explicit teaching is teaching in a very structured way that makes it clear what the target behavior is through use of examples, modeling, and practice. The specific steps of explicit teaching include the following (Stormont et al., 2008; Stormont, Reinke, Herman, & Lembke, 2012):

★ Determine the specific appropriate behavior to teach.
★ Determine if the behavior has multiple subskills; for example "line up safely" could include the following subskills: (1) Put materials away at desk. (2) Push in chair. (3) Zero voice. (4) Walk to door.
★ Secure attention.
★ Introduce behavior and the importance of it.
★ Introduce a range of examples.
★ Use popular, respected peers and adults.
★ Use multiple examples to show what the behavior can look like.
★ Only the teacher models examples of what the behavior doesn't look like (we don't want students to practice the inappropriate behavior).
★ Use role-plays with students.
★ Prompt for use throughout the day.
★ Provide reinforcement for use throughout the day.
★ Assign homework.
★ Practice again the next day.
★ Reteach or provide more support for students who struggle with behavior.
★ Assess for maintenance.

Teachers can determine the behavior they will explicitly teach through the use of a matrix. As more and more schools in the United States are using SW-PBIS (www.pbis.org), many teachers are familiar with the matrix and behavior expectations. If schools are not using SW-PBIS, teachers can still determine the behaviors they want to teach and use the following format:

Expectations	Classroom-Specific Rules	Lunch-Specific Rules
Be respectful	Only use your things. Ask for help politely. Respect differences.	Push in chairs. Throw trash away. Listen to others.
Be safe	Use materials appropriately. Walk. Be where you should be.	Walk. Chew slowly. Report spills.
Be kind	Use kind words. Include others. Recognize others' success.	Say thank you to helpers. Help others. Keep hands to yourself.

It is also important to help students meet expectations that differ because of the requirements of the different settings, context, or content. To help students understand, teachers can post a matrix of expectations and provide the practice and feedback needed to establish the desired behaviors. Below is a simple matrix for a language arts period to set expectations for when to talk.

Language Arts
Whole group:
Raise your hand before talking.
Small group:
Use your inside voice.
Independent work:
Work quietly without talking.

Table 5.1 is a blank matrix that can be used to create your own expectations for your classroom. It can also be used for other nonclassroom settings such as the playground, bathroom, hallways, cafeteria, library, assemblies, when visiting other classes, field trips, and any other applicable setting.

USE PRECORRECTIVE STATEMENTS, PROMPTS, AND PROXIMITY

Precorrective statements are detailed statements that prompt students for the correct, appropriate behavior or routine prior to a specific activity or transition. Sometimes students practice the correct behavior or routine within the context of these statements. In Chapter 4, these statements were referred to as previews. Once precorrective statements or previews have been presented for some time they can be replaced with a cue (verbal or visual) or prompt to represent the taught behavior (e.g., attention cue). Later in this chapter, we will discuss how this can be used with praise for a powerful combination to support appropriate behavior.

Proximity is a strategy where physical closeness is used to remind students of what they are suppose to be doing. If a student is talking when that isn't part of the activity or engaging in other types of problem behavior, the teacher just moves and stands by the student. This can be used with cues for what they are suppose to be doing (redirection) or an on-the-spot practice opportunity (e.g., how to ask for assistance, access materials, etc.).

Table 5.1 Blank Matrix to Plan Social Skills

EXPECTATIONS	CLASSROOM	_____
	RULES:	RULES:
	RULES:	RULES:
	RULES:	RULES:

Teachers can also use praise statements directed at what students in close proximity to a student who is not engaging in appropriate behavior are doing. The purpose of these statements is to remind the student of what he or she should be doing. Sample statements include these:

★ I see John and Anthony have their papers out and are ready for writing.
★ Thanks for being ready for reading, Chloe and De Quan.
★ I see Table 1 is ready; people have their voices off and materials out. Table 2 is ready.

Teachers can also give rewards to students who are demonstrating appropriate behavior, which is discussed in the next section.

POSITIVE REINFORCEMENT

Positive reinforcement is the increase of a specific behavior following receiving a specific response for that behavior. Punishment is the decrease of a specific behavior following a specific response for that behavior. Often, teachers fall into the trap of providing attention for problem behavior; even if this attention is viewed as negative and therefore considered a punishment, if the student's behavior increases, then this is actually positive reinforcement of the behavior through negative attention. What teachers need to do is focus on providing positive attention for positive behavior. Often, teachers need to plan to do this and have specific reminders to "catch students being good."

Specific praise statements are the best type of positive reinforcement to try first for several reasons. First, these statements can serve to support teaching specific social skills because they provide detailed feedback. Second, they can build positive relationships between the teacher and student. Third, they don't cost anything and can be used anywhere. But some students do not find these statements reinforcing, and this is clearly seen when students engage in problem behavior following such a statement.

Examples of specific praise statements for specific behaviors listed in the previous matrix include the following:

★ I heard how politely you asked for help, Philip; you said "please" and used a calm tone of voice. That was very respectful.
★ Nice work pushing in your chair, Jackson. That was very respectful.
★ I see you walking to the door, Michelle. Nice job that is very safe.
★ That was very kind of you to help Sally clean up her mess.
★ I heard you thank Mrs. Miller. Nice use of kind words.

It is very powerful to combine precorrective statements with behavior-specific praise statements (Conroy, Sutherland, Haydon, Stormont, & Harmon, 2009). It is also important to stress that if teachers aren't using these strategies, then they need to plan to do this and monitor if they did use the strategies they planned to use (Stormont & Reinke, 2009). An example of a planning sheet is shown in Table 5.2, and Table 5.3 is a blank form.

Group Rewards

Especially when more than one child is at risk in a classroom, group contingencies are very effective in supporting positive behavior. When using group contingencies, the teacher targets a behavior that the group needs to work on and then targets goals for improvement. Some examples include improving on (a) lining up at recess the first time asked, (b) specific lunchroom behavior, (c) participating appropriately in a large group, (c) helping peers when they need help, and (d) completing math fact sheets quickly and accurately. It is important that classroom-level rewards are affordable, easy, and brief (Stormont et al., 2012). Some examples include the following (Stormont et al., 2012):

★ Five to 10 minutes of free time
★ Chatting with a neighbor for a few minutes
★ Making silly faces or silly sounds
★ Playing a quick game the kids like to play
★ Singing a song
★ Doing a dance to a song
★ Getting stickers
★ Doing the Hokey Pokey

Table 5.2   Sample Planning Sheet for Precorrection and Praise

Specific Target Behavior	Planned Precorrective Statements	Planned Behavior Specific Praise
Lining up for lunch, recess, specials	It is time for _____. Remember to push your chair in, have zero voices, and walk to the door.	I see (insert who you want to acknowledge—a whole group or individual students or both) walking quietly to the door. Awesome job.
Asking for help in independent work	Remember when you are working, if you need my help, quietly raise your hand, and I will come as soon as possible.	Michael, thank you for raising your hand and waiting for me to come assist you.

Table 5.3 Planning Sheet for Precorrection and Praise

Specific Target Behavior	Planned Precorrective Statements	Planned Behavior-Specific Praise

Individual Rewards

Individual rewards are essential to support some children in their behavior change. For individual rewards to be effective, they must be delivered immediately following the desired behavior and associated with that behavior (contingent upon). If they are positive reinforcers for a child and delivered in this manner, they will increase the frequency of the specific target behavior (Alberto & Troutman, 2011). Teachers can determine what is a potential positive reinforcer by getting to know the child. It is very important to choose reinforcers that are actually reinforcing! And it is important to remember that children can tire of reinforcers if they are offered too frequently or even just because children's interests and needs change. Teachers can also develop surveys (like the consensogram presented in Chapter 2 but have children stick their names on specific choices such as candy). Or they can develop reinforcer menus where they list a set of potential reinforcers and children rate how much they would like to earn each specific reward on a scale of 1 to 9 (Alberto & Troutman, 2011). Teachers can also use existing tools and surveys to help them identify children's preferences. Listed below are a few apps, websites, and articles to help teachers identify reinforcers that will be effective for individual children.

★ Preference and Reinforcer Assessment is an app designed by a board-certified behavior analyst and offered in the iTunes store to help teachers and others gather data to determine the best reinforcers for a student: https://itunes.apple.com/us/app/preference-reinforcer-assessment/id436692530?mt=8

★ Jackpot! Reinforcement Survey Generator is an online tool for creating individualized reinforcement inventories provided by Intervention Central, a website designed to provide free assessment and intervention tools to educators. Furthermore, besides offering suggestions for academic and nonacademic reinforcers, and tangibles and edibles, Jackpot provides reinforcement options that can be linked to the function of a behavior, such as peer or adult attention and escape from nonpreferred activities: http://www.jimwrightonline.com/php/jackpot/jackpot.php

★ The Center for Effective Collaboration and Practice website offers a model of a forced-choice reinforcement inventory (Cartwright & Cartwright, 1970) modified by Gable (1991) that helps teachers identify the kinds of reinforcers children prefer, such as consumables or peer approval, and again helps teachers match children's preferences to the function of a behavior: http://cecp.air.org/fba/problembehavior3/appendixc.htm

For teachers to use reinforcement effectively, children must have choice, and teachers can use tools such as those offered above to identify children's preferences. However, while choice and preference are important, the section that follows provides critical information about the need to match reinforcement to the function of the behavior.

DETERMINING FUNCTION

When children demonstrate problem behavior that doesn't respond to simple supports, it is important to determine what may be supporting their behavior. This is referred to as the function for their behavior. Typically, children will engage in behavior to gain something or to escape something. Often, what children are trying to gain is attention (e.g., from teachers, peers); what they are trying to escape is often a challenging task, work, or specific setting (e.g., work with peers). It is important to ask guiding questions such as what happens right before the behavior and what happens right after the behavior? What happens right before the behavior could be the trigger for the behavior. What happens right after could be what is reinforcing the behavior. There are many quick A-B-C sheets available for teachers to use to collect information on the function of children's behavior. These represent the before (**A**ntecedent), the behavior (**B**ehavior), and the consequence for the behavior (**C**onsequence).

Examples follow:

Example 1

Antecedent	Behavior	Consequence
Teacher asks Jon to get out his writing journal	Jon yells	Teacher ignores
Five minutes later, teacher asks Jon to get out his writing work	Jon yells again	Teacher sends him to the office

Example 2

Antecedent	Behavior	Consequence
Teacher is reading a book in large group	Sandra blurts out a funny comment	Her peers laugh at her comment
Teacher continues to read	Sandra blurts out another comment about the book	Peers laugh Teacher sends her to the safe seat

What is most likely supporting Jon's negative behavior (yelling) in the first example? It is highly likely he is trying to escape writing. Once the teacher knows this, he or she can use an appropriate intervention from this chapter to support him in doing his writing. Precorrection, praise, finding incentives, and the PASS system (Stormont et al., 2012) described later would all be appropriate.

For Example 2, what is supporting Sandra's behavior? She seems to like peer attention and maybe even the teacher's negative attention during reading. Interventions such as precorrection, praise, individual incentives, and proximity would be good places to start with Sandra.

CHANGING SETTING FACTORS

After considering the function of the behavior for children, it is important to then change factors in the environment that may be supporting the behavior. For example, maybe information collected indicates that a specific peer is often a trigger; the change to the setting would be to move the peer farther away or to teach the peer not to be a trigger. As another example, perhaps every time children are asked to line up from recess one child gets very angry and often gets sent to the office because of it. In this case, teaching the playground supervisors to provide this child a prompt five minutes before the transition would be a good strategy to try first.

For Jon and Sandra in the former examples, some setting factors could be modified. Jon could be given a chance to work on his journal with an agreed-upon peer if he has problems getting started or just likes working with others. He could also be given prompts before to get him ready. For Sandra, the teacher could have her sit right in front and cue her to raise her hand and only say appropriate comments (those about the book). The teacher could also prompt the other students to refrain from laughing at off-task comments during reading time.

Give Them a Break: PASS

If children's behavior is to escape a setting, one promising strategy is to teach them how to appropriately ask for and use a break pass. Developed by Wendy Reinke (Stormont et al., 2012) at the University of Missouri, the PASS system is a system where a child gets to take a pass a specific number of times every day to get out of an activity he or she doesn't like. The system must be used in a structured way. The point is to teach students how to "escape" challenging tasks in a more appropriate manner and then reward their efforts in taking fewer and fewer passes and remediating their skill deficits in tasks they try to avoid. Dr. Reinke gives the following details to support teachers in their planning when using the PASS (Stormont et al., 2012):

★ When is it OK to use a pass? Targeting the specific problem times is a good idea.
★ What does the student do after using a pass? It is important to have something planned for the student to do such as using preferred activities that still build on academic skills.
★ What visual representation is used for the PASS?
★ What process will be used for the student to indicate that he or she wants to use a pass? It is important that this is specific and taught to the student.
★ What if the student uses all passes and still avoids work? It is important to have a system in place that rewards students for completing a certain amount of work and using fewer passes over time. Students can earn points if they don't take a pass and lose points if they refuse to complete a specific amount of work. It is always important to meet students where they are and set appropriate goals for work completion (a little more work completed over time versus 100% of work completed).

Take a Break

Another suggested strategy for children who demonstrate problem behavior to avoid work is to teach them to request a break. It is important to teach students who are engaging in problem behavior to request a break in a calm manner and then have plans for where they will go, how many times they can request a break, and what they will do in the break area (Stormont et al., 2012). The break area could include prompts or written forms students can complete as they try to problem solve and calm down. It is also good to include things to help them monitor how they are feeling and to help them calm down. Anger thermometers can help children register their feelings (On a scale of 1 to 10, I am at a 7 for anger or an 8 for sadness) and then use strategies to help themselves calm down. As Dr. Reinke notes when describing the specific steps for this strategy, it is important that children receive social skills interventions to use while they are taking a break. Once children take a break, it is also important to teach students how to return to the class setting (a statement could be good). Then the teacher should positively reinforce the student for making the choice to take a break instead of being disruptive and make sure the student gets involved in what the class is doing in a positive manner.

CHAPTER SUMMARY

The importance of teaching social behavior skills cannot be overstated. Children with poor social skills are at risk for numerous negative outcomes, including teacher and peer rejection. In this chapter, evidence-based strategies for teaching and supporting the use of appropriate social skills were discussed. It is vital that teachers attend to what function the behavior may be serving for a child so an appropriate intervention can be matched accordingly. Strategies presented in this chapter are free and simple to use but may take time and planning to use them systematically. The chapter also includes many examples and planning tools to support teachers' use of strategies.

6 Use Simple Supports for Improving Academic Success

One of our goals for this book is to provide general educators, as well as others who work with children at risk, specific strategies they can use tomorrow with their students. However, it is still important to understand why specific strategies are important to use and to use them consistently to determine if they are effective. The following framework should guide the use of the supports provided in this chapter.

FRAMEWORK FOR SUCCESS

1. Consider children's characteristics from Chapter 1 that are creating risk for failure in a specific lesson, unit, or setting.

2. Use principles of Universal Design for Learning to differentiate instruction and provide access to the general curriculum for all learners (Chapter 7).

3. Using data (see Chapter 3), determine how to meet children at risk where they are and move them forward in the curriculum or skill they are working on.

4. Use only research-grounded practices.

5. Provide extra individualized supports based on specific characteristics.

6. Use data to monitor progress and to set goals (Chapter 3).

It is important that teachers use their time wisely to support learning and only *use practices with a research-based foundation.* In this chapter,
we focus on specific research-grounded practices that can be integrated
easily into the general education classroom. It is also important for teachers to consider children's characteristics and learning needs in the design
phase of curriculum development. One recent framework for curriculum
design and implementation is Universal Design for Learning. According
to the National Center on Universal Design for Learning (UDL; 2012a),
"Universal Design for Learning is a set of principles for curriculum development that give all individuals equal opportunities to learn." UDL is
defined and included in current educational law and policy (Atkins et al.,
2010). UDL asks teachers to consider equitable access to the curriculum
before designing or selecting curriculum in order to be sure that the curriculum will not pose barriers to learning. UDL gives teachers guidance
in how to identify the instructional goals, materials, methods, and assessments that promote success for diverse learners, including students at
risk. Key principles of UDL support teachers in ensuring that teaching
offers *multiple means of representation, multiple means of action and expression,*
and *multiple means of engagement* (National Center on Universal Design for
Learning, 2012b). To help teachers differentiate their instruction, these key
principles and the individual checkpoints supporting each principle in
the UDL guidelines provide a structured framework for making curriculum more inclusive. A wealth of resources to support UDL implementation and to access current research on UDL are available at the National
Center on Universal Design for Learning website (http://www.udlcenter
.org) and at the Center for Applied Special Technology, or CAST, website
(http://www.cast.org).

Especially for children at risk, teachers should carefully identify and
implement the research-based practices and interventions that match
students' learning characteristics and promote the principles of UDL to
support learning.

RESEARCH-BASED PRACTICES
FOR SUPPORTING LEARNERS AT RISK

Secure Prior Knowledge. Many children who are at risk for failure have very
limited background knowledge in specific areas. Sometimes this happens
because they have attention or memory problems and didn't learn the

information when presented. Other times it is because they have moved to a new school or have missed the content in the curriculum. Also, sometimes children don't have the same background knowledge as other children given they haven't had the same experiences, such as traveling, visiting museums, and other types of enrichment-related experiences (Espinosa, 2005). Teachers can have children discuss what they know about specific topics or give a pretest to determine prior knowledge. Teachers can fill in some gaps in prior knowledge through showing videos illustrating the topic or creating centers in the classroom that represent what is being taught and include music, materials, and other artifacts to represent the topic (Stormont, 2007). For example, if children haven't been to the ocean or to a rain forest or to a farm, a teacher could make a center that represents this topic.

Explicit Instruction. As stated in Chapter 5, explicit instruction is a highly effective practice for all students and is essential for students who are at risk for failure. The same steps of explicit instruction outlined to teach social behavior also apply to academic behavior.

Determine Instructional Level. Through the use of systematic assessment, teachers can determine where students are in terms of their skills and comprehension and then find an appropriate instructional level. This was discussed in Chapter 3.

Cognitive Learning Strategies. Cognitive learning strategies are also very effective for supporting learning. These are helpful because of the various characteristics learners who are at risk for failure have that affect processing and learning information. These types of strategies engage learners in reviewing material before they begin to determine what they already know about a topic and what the main ideas of the topic are; they also engage learners in interacting with the material while reading and when reflecting on what they learned (Bos & Vaughn, 2006; Stormont, 2007).

★ What do I know?
★ What do I want to learn?
★ What have I learned?
★ What remaining questions do I have?

Graphic Organizers. Other strategies to increase the concreteness and meaningfulness of content include graphic organizers. They can be used in combination with cognitive learning strategies where children create visual representations of what they already **k**now about a topic, followed by what they **w**ant to know about a topic, and then what they **l**earned about a topic (K-W-L strategy; Vaughn & Bos, 2009). For children with memory problems, impulsivity, attention problems, or motivational problems, these can be powerful tools to increase interest and engagement with the content. Graphic organizers can support students in brainstorming and retrieving what they know about a topic or help them organize thoughts before writing. Venn diagrams are also very helpful for showing how two things are alike and unique for comparing and contrasting. Sequence organizers are good to support learning a concept that occurs in a sequence (e.g., water cycle stages) or the events that took place in a story. Some helpful websites with multiple examples of different graphic organizers as well as forms teachers can complete for their own lessons include the following:

http://my.hrw.com/nsmedia/intgos/html/igo.htm

http://www.eduplace.com/graphicorganizer/

http://www.edhelper.com/teachers/General_graphic_organizers.htm

Teachers can also develop their own graphic organizers to match content using technology. Wikipedia has a list of free and paid options (http://en.wikipedia.org/wiki/List_of_concept-_and_mind-mapping_software) for concept mapping software and applications. Furthermore, asking children to create a graphic organizer about a specific topic is an effective way to assess what a child knows and how he or she is organizing the information (Jonassen, Reeves, Hong, Harvey, & Peters, 1997; McArthur Capizzi & Barton-Arwood, 2009).

Increase Practice With peers and in Small Groups. As discussed in Chapter 3, one of the simplest supports we can provide children at risk is to systematically plan more practice opportunities.

INDIVIDUALIZE BASED ON SPECIFIC CHARACTERISTICS

Even when teachers use research-grounded practices, some children will need more individualized supports. In this section, individualized supports for specific characteristics of children who are at risk for failure (discussed in Chapter 1) are presented. But it is important to stress that teachers need to be systematic about providing supports. Here is an example of an individualized support plan:

Student/Characteristics	Supports
David Impulsivity Memory problems	Frequent reminders before challenging settings A visual cue on desk to remind of the daily routine and what he should be doing

A blank planning form is included in Table 6.1. Also, some ideas to support children with ADHD with simple supports are presented in Table 6.2. For example, following is a sample form for using simple supports using sticky notes and highlighters (Stormont, 2008; Zentall, 2006).

Select	Who will I use this with?
1. Use sticky notes to highlight what to do first, second, and third on any assignment.	Jackson, during reading

Attention Problems

Children with attention problems often need support coming to attention, selectively attending to the right thing, and sustaining attention (Barkley, 1995, 2005; Stormont, 2007; Zentall, 2005, 2006).

Coming to Attention. It is important to always secure all students' attention before providing instructions or teaching. Teachers can use many attention signals:

★ Turning the lights on and off
★ Clapping hands (teacher claps alone or claps a specific sequence and children clap a sequence back)
★ Saying part of a word or sentence and the students complete the word or sentence (The teacher says, "I say *Right*, you say *Now*" and pauses before continuing, then says explicitly "**RIGHT** . . . you say" and then waits for children to say *Now*)
★ Turning on music
★ Raising a hand or using another physical cue

For children with problems coming to attention, it would be good to use them as leaders in securing students' attention. In a class with class jobs, this could be their job.

Selective Attention. Children with selective attention problems need support focusing their attention. They need teachers and peers to highlight what they should be attending to and in what order they should be completing tasks (Stormont, 2008; Zentall, 2006). Simple supports teachers could use include highlighting (or having the student highlight) directions, using index cards or Post-it notes to outline steps for completing tasks (first, do this; second, do this; third, do this), or using additional visual prompts outlining what to do that are laminated and on students' desks or in their folders (e.g., steps for figuring out how to spell words, sentence

Table 6.1 Individualization Support Plan

Student/Characteristics	Supports

Table 6.2   Simple Supports Using Sticky Notes and Highlighters

Select	Who will I use this with?
Use sticky notes to highlight what to do first, second, and third on any assignment.	
Use different colors of highlighters to indicate what to do first and second in assignments.	
Use a sticky note to prompt them to check spelling when they are finished.	
Work a problem on a sticky note with a peer or teacher and then use it as an example of how to execute a specific type of problem.	
Create an order for completing tasks and then highlight when each one is completed.	
Create estimated times for completion of homework and then put ETC on a sticky note with the time on it.	
Have different color sticky notes for things to take home and things to bring back to school.	
Use sticky notes to create graphic organizers, including sequence charts.	
Have children write down thoughts and questions on sticky notes as others are talking or reading.	
Give a number of sticky notes as free movement passes.	

Source: Stormont (2008); Zentall (2006).

starters, etc.). It is also important to spend extra time with students so they understand main ideas, including why they are doing specific things and how it connects to a larger unit. Often, students with attention problems also have difficulty reengaging once distracted, and teachers need to have an attention cue for students to get back to work (Barkley, 1995; Zentall, 2005, 2006).

Sustain Attention. Sydney Zentall's extensive research in this area can be used to address additional specific supports that children with ADHD may need to sustain attention to tasks and teaching, including the following strategies for how to set up the classroom environment:

★ Make sure the environment is stimulating especially when children are practicing repetitive, boring content.
★ Add stimulation such as highlighting the end of a reading passage to sustain interest to the reading and foster comprehension.
★ Understand that children are drawn to novel, stimulating activities and things, so make sure to add novelty to tasks, especially those that are rote or repetitive.
★ Use games and fun materials to increase sustaining attention to tasks.
★ Use peer and small-group work.
★ Use technology.
★ Plan choices.
★ Intersperse practice throughout the day rather than having students practice something for 30 minutes (e.g., handwriting or spelling); break that into three 10-minute practice sessions.
★ Give fewer but more challenging problems so students can demonstrate knowledge but not have to complete 30 problems.
★ Break down large assignments into smaller parts and give one part at a time instead of the entire assignment.

Memory Problems

Many children struggle due to problems learning new information (short-term memory) and remembering what they have learned (long-term memory). The other characteristics presented in this chapter also influence children's ability to remember information, and the supports listed here are good for other problems as well (e.g., attention). Children with memory problems benefit from the following (Stormont, 2007):

★ Provide concrete representations of problems to be solved.
★ Provide as many external memory supports as possible—for example, reminders of the steps to use to solve a problem or steps listed to remember to go back through work to check spelling and so on.

The sample support card in the next section on impulsivity would also support children with memory problems.

★ Use specific cues for what children need to do during transitions, including previews and precorrective statements, discussed in other chapters.

★ Provide visual representations of steps to use to solve a specific type of problem or to support ideas to write about and so on.

★ For long-term memory problems, graphic organizers (discussed in this chapter) are helpful organizers of key information.

★ Use frequent review of material to support maintenance.

★ Use assistive technology to complete the lower-level tasks and enable students to focus all cognitive efforts on higher-level thinking (e.g., spell-checkers, text-to-speech applications, and calculators all can provide access to the full curriculum; see Bouck & Flanagan, 2009; Edyburn, 2007).

Impulsivity

A long time ago, Mr. Rogers, who was featured on a famous television program designed for younger children, sang a song about *finding something to do while you're waiting.* Many children who are at risk struggle to do this, and we need to increase support in the settings in which they struggle. Essentially with impulsive children, we need to help them find something to do while they wait, including having visual cards with options of what they can do while they are waiting for help or for a new task. Such a card could look like this:

What can I do when I wait?
➢ Work on my spelling words
➢ Work on my math facts
➢ Write in my journal
➢ Ask my approved peer for help

It is also important for children to monitor their impulsive responses. Children can monitor (by counting) how many times they speak when it isn't their turn or when they weren't called on (also known as impulsivity training). Then children can set goals for improving their behavior (Stormont, Reinke, Herman, & Lembke, 2012). When children do blurt out something unrelated to the activity at hand, teachers can redirect them to the current task but place their idea on a card, Post-it note, laminated board, or other display and refer to it as a "parking lot" (Stormont, 2007; Zentall, 2006). Then during community-building time or some time during the day, the ideas that were in the parking lot to be discussed later can be discussed. For example, if David blurts out something related to his birthday party during math time the teacher could quickly say, "David we are working on math now, but I am going to write down David's birthday on this note and put it in our parking lot for later." Once children understand the parking lot idea, all the teacher may have to say is, "David, math now, but your birthday is going in the parking lot for later."

For children who are impulsive, it is critical to understand how impulsivity influences how they will work for rewards. If children are offered a reward for doing something (especially something hard), the reward needs to be immediate! Even if it is a small reward (Jolly Rancher candy, sticker), this will work much better for impulsive children than something that is offered at the end of the week, even if it seems like a much better reward (Barkley, 1995; Zentall, 2006).

It is also important to use the Premack principle (if . . . then; Zentall, 2006) to work with impulsive behavior. This has also been referred to as the dessert principle (if you eat your vegetables, then you can have dessert). A visual could also be used to help children see that if they do something specific, then they receive a specific reward. This could be displayed on a sheet of paper on the child's desk like a contract with IF spelled on the top left-hand column and THEN displayed on the right-hand column. Then the behaviors and rewards that are agreed upon with the teacher and student could be written or drawn in the columns below the IF and THEN.

Hyperactivity

Especially when children are younger, teachers need to plan a lot of movement into lessons. Then, as they get older, some children will still need to move more than others. Teachers need to understand that this is a physical trait (like height or IQ) and not something children have much control over (Stormont, 2007; Zentall, 2006). Thus, activity needs should be supported. If children have needs to move due to hyperactivity, whether they have ADHD or just elevated activity needs, teachers can use one of the following strategies:

★ Give children something to quietly manipulate while they work or listen.

★ Allow children to stand while working or listening.
★ Include movement in lessons and during transitions.
★ Allow many helper jobs that include movement (passing out papers, taking notes to other teachers, taking attendance to the office, etc.).
★ Have children walk and talk more, including clarifying assignment details and that they are on the right track with the teacher or a peer. This supports attention and impulsivity needs as well.
★ NEVER take away recess! That would be like not feeding a child lunch and then expecting him or her to learn.

Organization Problems

Children with organizational problems tend to struggle in both object organization and time/planning organization (Stormont, 2007; Stormont et al., 2012; Zentall, 2006; Zentall, Harper, & Stormont-Spurgin, 1993). For object organization, it is important to teach children routines so they can retrieve what they need to fairly quickly. For time/planning organization, it is important that children receive support with time estimation and planning.

Object Support

★ Support children in developing routines for object placement. For example, a homework basket could be used in class, and homework could be collected at the very beginning of the day.
★ Homework could be clearly marked in folders with comments like "Bring Back to School."
★ Children could have a few minutes each day to organize their desks with prompts provided for where things go:
    ★ "Organization time! Take a minute to . . ."
        ☆ Clean your area
        ☆ Put away papers to take home
        ☆ Wipe off desk, if needed
        ☆ Clean floor around you, if needed
★ Children could have reminders of what they should always have in their backpack. For example, "Do you have your . . ."
    ★ Pencils?
    ★ Homework folder?
    ★ Writing journal?
★ Children could have sheets or prompt cards to remind them of what needs to go home and what needs to come back. An example may look like the following:

TAKE HOME	BRING BACK
Book order	Lunch money
Homework	Homework

Time/Planning Support

★ Use explicit instruction to teach students how to use the clock and calendars to monitor their time management toward goal completion.

★ Create a daily activity schedule. Use pictures, and for English learners, pair primary language with English and pictures.

★ Use checklists and rubrics to help students finish work and evaluate the quality of their work.

★ Practice sequencing.

★ Break down larger assignments into smaller ones.

★ Do a task analysis to help students complete one step at a time and check off steps as they complete them.

★ Help students estimate how long certain tasks will take and provide feedback on their estimations.

★ In the eKidskills (http://kidtools.org/See_eKidSkills.php) and iKidSkills (http://kidtools.org/See_iKidSkills.php) sections, the Kid Coach: The Kidtools Support Systems website (http://kidtools.org) includes tools for doing homework (such as a homework and long-term planners and a schedule maker), getting organized (such as an assignment card and backpack organizer), and test preparation strategies.

★ The Skills for School Success program (Archer & Gleason, 1993) is a research-based program that uses an explicit instructional approach and includes teacher training materials, scripted teacher lesson plans, and student booklets to teach organizational skills and school behaviors such as keeping a calendar, completing homework, proofreading, reading actively, taking notes, and communicating effectively (http://www.curriculumassociates.com/products/detail.aspx?title=SkillsSS).

★ The James Madison University Learning Toolbox (http://coe.jmu.edu/Learningtoolbox/) is a free online resource for mnemonic strategies to help students with organizational, study, and learning skills (such as keeping a calendar, remembering what to bring home, setting goals, taking tests, organizing information, etc.). This site provides teacher supports, including background information about strategy instruction and materials on how to use strategies effectively.

Motivation

Many children have difficulty with being motivated to learn. Often, children need incentives to learn, but the goal of teachers should always be to increase children's interest in learning for learning sake (intrinsic motivation). Strategies to increase interest in learning include the following:

★ Get to know students' interests and tie those interests into lessons.
★ Make sure to know the skill levels of students and that there is an appropriate instructional match.
★ Build success.
★ Intersperse difficult problems with easier problems (Belfiore et al., 2005).
★ Create an expertise for every student who is at risk, emphasizing his or her strengths.
★ Teach goal setting and monitoring goals to increase the ability to connect success with effort.

CHAPTER SUMMARY

This chapter presented a framework for supporting children at risk for academic failure. It is important that children's specific characteristics are considered and instruction is differentiated accordingly. Individualized supports also help children be more successful, and teachers should plan to use these supports systematically. It is also imperative that data (Chapter 3) guide decision making about goals and progress and that only research-based practices are used to support academic growth. Many research-based strategies were presented in this chapter that teachers could easily use to support children's academic growth.

7 Use Technology

★ Do you enjoy using technology for teaching and learning? Do you feel confident in trying new technology?

★ What technology do you have easy access to in your school?

★ Is technology professional development available? Are there ongoing technology supports?

★ What technology are you currently using? Does it meet your instructional objectives?

★ What are some learning problems or instructional objectives that you have not been able to meet using your own best practices without technology?

Technology is constantly changing, and this chapter provides teachers with information to help them make decisions about choosing technology, along with resources for information to help them keep pace with what is available. Technology has properties, or affordances (Gibson, 1977), that enable teachers and their students to accomplish things that would not be possible without it. To be successful in today's world, teachers and students need to become literate users of technology. For children at risk, teachers have a special responsibility to promote digital literacy because just as there are gaps between opportunities and outcomes for these students academically and socially, there is also a digital divide. Children at risk are the technological "have nots" with less computer and Internet access available in their homes and, frequently, inequitable access in their schools too (Moore, Laffey, Espinosa, & Lodree, 2002). Teachers must provide increased access during the school day to help children at risk keep pace with their more advantaged peers.

WHAT IS TECHNOLOGY

First of all, *what is technology?* Technology can be thought of as a category of scientific knowledge for problem solving, along with the machines or tools created to meet those goals. Educational technology is technology applied to impact learning outcomes.

In education, technology can be thought of in a few ways. First, it can be considered educational or instructional. Next, it could be considered either remedial or compensatory. For students with disabilities, technology can also be assistive. Furthermore, technology can be low tech, mid tech, or high tech. *However, technology is not magic; effective implementation and the quality of learning outcomes rely on the leadership of school personnel and the teachers who guide its use.* Well-chosen technology in conjunction with evidence-based instructional methods and practices and sound, clear instructional objectives has the potential to significantly enhance learning outcomes (Clark, 1994). Technology can strengthen teaching and learning (Aziz, 2010).

Below are some definitions and information about kinds of technology, categories of technology, and frameworks for implementing technology in schools. Within these definitions, there is important information about technology in educational law and policy that every teacher should know.

★ **Accessible instructional materials (AIM):** According to the National Center on Accessible Instructional Materials (http://aim. cast.org/learn/accessiblemedia/allaboutaim), "Accessible instructional materials, or AIM, are materials that are designed or converted in a way that makes them usable across the widest range of student variability regardless of format (print, digital, graphical, audio, video). IDEA (Individuals with Disabilities Education Act) specifically focuses on accessible formats of print instructional materials. In relation to IDEA, the term AIM refers to print instructional materials that have been transformed into the specialized formats of Braille, large print, audio, or digital text."

★ **Assistive technology (AT):** The Assistive Technology Act of 2004 defines an *assistive technology device* in the following way: "Any item, piece of equipment, or product system, whether acquired commercially, modified, or customized, that is used to increase, maintain, or improve functional capabilities of individuals with disabilities." Under the Individuals with Disabilities Education Act (IDEA), as part of the Individualized Education Program (IEP) process, students with disabilities are entitled to be matched with assistive technology to reduce barriers to learning that are imposed by their disability and to receive assistive technology services that provide them with access to the general curriculum. Children at risk who are not identified as having disabilities are not eligible for AT support under current law; however, it is important for teachers to understand that technology can have assistive properties and enable a child to perform tasks or engage in learning that would not be possible without it. Teachers can match technology to the needs of at-risk learners to circumvent barriers to learning. For example, for a child with poor math fluency, providing a calculator during word problem solving instruction will allow the child to focus his or her cognitive energy on the higher-level task, and for children who are dysfluent readers, access to digital text supports the development of comprehension.

★ **Educational and instructional technology:** Educational and instructional technologies are applications of technology that are either designed expressly for or selected to promote teaching and learning. These technologies should be developed (and implemented) based on sound learning theory and informed by knowledge from cognitive and social sciences (the learning sciences). Well-designed and well-chosen educational and instructional technology considers the human capacity for memory and attention. Technology influences learning in both internal and external ways, given its potential to support and enhance memory, perception, and cognition, along with its capacity to enable learners to demonstrate their learning in meaningful ways. Teachers should have clear instructional objectives in mind when choosing and using technology, including plans for assessment of outcomes.

★ **Compensatory and remedial purposes:** For students with disabilities and students at risk, technology can also serve compensatory or remedial purposes. Compensatory technology is the analog for assistive technology for students who do not have a disability and therefore are not protected by IDEA. In this case, the technology is used to differentiate instruction or as an accommodation for students who would benefit from the supports. Using low-tech examples, for a student who struggles with subitizing, manipulatives provide concrete representations of how many items are in a group, and for an English learner, to support vocabulary development, pictures with labels in primary language aid learning.

Technology can also provide remediation for skill gaps and knowledge deficits common in children with or at risk for disabilities. Students with or at risk for disabilities may require much more practice and many more opportunities to respond than a typically developing peer in order to learn new information or acquire a new skill, along with more systematic and frequent review in order to maintain learning (see Chapter 4). High-quality computer programs can provide practice and even feedback to students, often using game formats that are much more engaging and motivating than paper-and-pencil drill.

★ **Low tech, mid tech, and high tech:** Technology is often expensive and requires training and maintenance to be useful. For these reasons, teachers should consider these factors in identifying technology for themselves and their students. Low-tech devices include the simplest and often least expensive options. They are generally not electronic, and examples might include a pencil grip, a large print book, or a highlighter. Mid-tech devices are more sophisticated but still easy to operate and moderately priced. Examples of these might include computer software for magnification or scanning, an audiobook, or a portable or adapted keyboard. High-tech devices are electronically sophisticated and can be quite expensive. Examples include accessibility software and applications (apps) such as text to speech/speech to text, word prediction, data management, and concept mapping tools, and devices such as computers and handhelds, such as enlargers, tablets and other smart devices. Augmentative and alternative communication (AAC) tools can be apps, software, or devices. These cross-platform options will increase as technology continues to innovate. In choosing technology, the simplest, most cost-effective option that will solve the problem or meet the need well is the best choice. Save the high-tech purchases for technology that meets either a very broad range of needs and purposes—and will therefore be useful by many people, for many purposes, and possibly even in many settings—or for a highly specific need that cannot be addressed in another way. Expensive options should have longevity, and both training needs and requirements for maintenance and technology support should be carefully considered. In some cases, expensive, and even temperamental, high-tech equipment is necessary to meet very specialized needs such as reading software for children with print disabilities, AAC devices for children with speech capacity that is less than their cognitive capacity to communicate, or a power wheelchair for a student with a physical impairment.

★ **Universal Design for Learning** (UDL; see Chapter 6)**:** The developers of UDL have, since its inception, had a strong focus on the potential for technology to provide access. In selecting technology, the Center for Applied Special Technology (CAST) recommends maintaining the focus on the learners' needs while keeping the learning goals in the forefront as you plan, implement, and evaluate. In a UDL classroom the technology may be required by some and preferred by others, but ideally, it is available to all. For example, for a student with a print disability, listening to an audiobook may be assistive (e.g., in UDL, multiple means of representation, options for perception), but for a peer, listening to an audiobook may be a preference (multiple means of engagement, options for recruiting interest), while for yet another student, the audiofile may help him or her to persist in a nonpreferred task (multiple means of engagement, options for sustaining effort and persistence). Technology is a powerful medium, and when the technology has been carefully chosen and employed by teachers, it can have strong positive impacts on motivation and learning. The UDL guidelines provide teachers with a structured framework for thinking about how to be more inclusive of the diverse learners in today's classrooms. To access the UDL guidelines, including definitions, examples, and recommendations for use, see http://www.udlcenter.org/aboutudl/udlguidelines/.

★ **Technology integration:** Technology integration is a meshing of curriculum and technology to meet learning goals. Like UDL, the most effective technology integration occurs in the instructional design phase. Too often, technology is just an add-on to instruction or used to perform a task that can be done just as well without it, or it performs a function that everyone likes, but it has no learning outcome (Cuban, Kirkpatrick, & Peck 2001). Successful technology integration is an ongoing process, and it is not measured by how much technology is in the environment, but by *why* the technology is the environment, *how* it is being used for learning, and by the observable and measurable learning outcomes demonstrating improved outcomes for the task/content *with* technology.

★ **Communities of practice:** Traditional professional development, most typically, a one-time half- or full-day workshop for technology learning, has not been an effective support for teachers. To learn to integrate technology effectively, teachers need ongoing, individualized support over time (Zorfass & Rivero, 2005; see Table 7.1). In almost all cases, technology has a learning curve. Rarely does technology "come out of the box" and work perfectly for the intended purpose the first time. For this reason, many teachers have created collaborative communities with their peers for support. These online and school-based groups provide teachers with access to information, support, and informal and regular professional development opportunities. While integrating technology requires time and persistence, teachers (and their students) are motivated when the data demonstrate the impact of technology on learning.

★ **Selecting, matching, and critically evaluating technology for learning:** Technology changes quickly, and since it can be expensive, it is important for schools and teachers to choose wisely, investing in technology that serves many students and many purposes or meets a specific and critical need. Educational technology is most likely to be well integrated when it works reliably, requires limited maintenance, and lasts a long time! For assistive technology, during the IEP process, the IEP team may use a technology-matching process such as the SETT framework, which considers the student, the environment, the tasks, and the tools needed for the student to address the tasks (Zabala, 2010–2013), or the Functional Evaluation for Assistive Technology (FEAT; Raskind & Bryant, 2002) to

Table 7.1   Communities of Practice to Support Technology Integration

Resource	Descriptions	URL
Learn NC: Building and maintaining an online professional learning community	This webpage, part of the Learn NC program from the University of North Carolina at Chapel Hill School of Education provides suggestions and resources for establishing and maintaining an effective professional learning community (PLC).	http://www.learnnc.org/lp/pages/7012
Connected Educators	This resource is under development in response to the National Educational Technology Plan. The U. S. Department of Education has contracted with the American Institutes of Research and several other organizations to help educators establish and connect to online communities of practice and conduct research.	http://connectededucators.org/about/
International Society for Technology in Education	ISTE is a professional organization whose mission is to improve learning through technology integration. On its website, ISTE shares access to its National Educational Technology Standards (NETS) for teachers and students, ways to evaluate technology needs, and social media and special interest groups that provide resources and support for professional development.	http://www.iste.org/about-iste http://www.iste.org/connect/communities
Technology and Media Association of the Council for Exceptional Children	TAM is a professional organization that is division of the Council for Exceptional Children. TAM offers publications, products, and webinars to support professional development in using technology to improve participation and outcomes for students with disabilities and other diverse learners.	http://www.tamcec.org/publications/

identify the most efficient and effective assistive technology options. In the case of educational technologies, schools and teachers may be bewildered by the multitude of choices and the aggressive commercial marketing. Furthermore, because technology is engaging, there is a risk of selecting technology that either has a novelty factor that wears off in time, becoming less engaging, or that students like but that has limited or no educational benefit. To identify effective educational technology, teachers must spend time investigating current research, evidence-based practices, and reputable online reviews of technology for learning. In addition, data on student achievement prior to including technology, during training, and as students master the technology should be collected and evaluated to inform instruction.

An example that may help teachers understand how to select technology would be to consider Ms. Mathes's use of Wordle in Chapter 2. By itself, Wordle is not a technology with evidence that it works in education. As a matter of fact, its developers describe it as a toy (http://www.wordle.net)! But Ms. Mathes has clear instructional objectives in mind for using Wordle; she wants to create a sense of community by helping students *see* the main ideas in their discussion and highlight areas of their agreement, to create a bond. Furthermore, Ms. Mathes uses the student work samples as her evaluation for meeting her instructional objectives. Ms. Mathes has considered the principles of UDL for this activity and is using Wordle as a tool, just as she would use a worksheet, textbook, or manipulatives to engage students in content. With Wordle, she is able to achieve her instructional goal in an inclusive and inviting manner. Furthermore, a permanent product has been created that can be displayed as a reminder of the classroom culture and expectations.

Another similar technology, Wordsift (http://www.wordsift.com/site/theory), was designed and tested for an educational purpose, and is based on sound learning theory. Research evidence, which recommends previewing of vocabulary to support English language learners in developing academic language, was used to guide the development of Wordsift, and the technology itself is currently being investigated for this purpose. Interactive features include the ability to create a word cloud to identify high-frequency words; sorting features by subject area, least to rare, and alphabetically; a visual thesaurus; access to images and video to provide a context for the meaning; and sample model sentences. To use Wordsift, the student enters text, and a word cloud is generated, along with the other corresponding features. Users can click on any word in the entered text to make that word the focus of the visual thesaurus, images, video, and so on.

In both of these cases, use of technology can achieve desired learning outcomes, although Wordle was used as a tool by a teacher and Wordsift has been independently validated for use with English learners. So how can teachers make reliable decisions in choosing technology? Teachers can ask themselves the following questions in making technology decisions:

★ Does the stated purpose of the technology match the instructional objective?
★ Will the technology pose any barriers for at-risk learners?
★ Does the technology have any particular affordances or features that will improve learning and access to the curriculum for at-risk learners?
★ Does the website, producer, or company provide any research evidence that the technology works for at-risk children? Is that evidence believable? Why or why not?
★ Is there independent research that demonstrates the technology works for the intended purpose?
★ Is the cost, ease of use, and maintenance appropriate for the setting?
★ What supports will be needed to use the technology? Are they accessible?
★ What data will I use to determine that the technology serves its purpose? Ideally, teachers should first collect evidence of students' performance without technology.
★ Once the technology is implemented, what is my plan for collecting more data to determine if my objectives have been achieved?

Finally, remember that technology is most powerful when we use it to achieve something that would take longer, be more difficult, or not be possible without it. A simple example is to think of eyeglasses as a low-tech form of assistive technology; for the second author, I would not be able to read and it would not be legal for me to drive without mine! In identifying learning goals, consider using technology for those that in the past have been difficult to achieve, particularly for at-risk students.

ACCESSING TECHNOLOGY

As we have discussed before, technology can be expensive, and children at risk are the least likely to have access to the latest and greatest. Urban and rural schools and schools in high-poverty areas in general are the least likely to have sufficient connectivity, hardware and software, and trained personnel. Children at risk have significantly less out-of-school access than do their middle-class peers. So given the expense, the maintenance, the training, and the professional development required to bring schools into the Digital Age, what can districts, schools, and teachers do to find resources?

★ Districts can contact their State Educational Technology Director (http://www.setda.org/web/guest/partner)
★ Districts can identify state resources for assistive technology on the National Assistive Technology Assistance Partnership Website (http://www.resnaprojects.org/nattap/at/stateprograms.html) or through the Association of Assistive Technology Act Programs website (http://www.ataporg.org)
★ Local universities with teacher education, library science, and information technology departments and programs may be interested in partnering with schools to support technology integration.
  ★ To find out about school and university partnerships in your state, check the National Network for Educational Renewal (http://www.nnerpartnerships.org/about-us/)
★ International, national, and local technology corporations may have grant, scholarship, or other outreach programs; check their websites and contact a representative for information.
  ★ For example, Cisco Systems (http://csr.cisco.com/pages/product-grant-program), Adobe Systems Incorporated (http://www.adobe.com/corporate-responsibility/product-software-donation.html), and Microsoft Corporation (http://www.microsoft.com/about/corporatecitizenship/en-us/nonprofits/) all have funding opportunities.
★ Many private and nonprofit foundations have an interest in and supports for increasing innovation and technology integration in schools.
  ★ A well-known example might include the Bill and Melinda Gates Foundation (http://www.gatesfoundation.org/How-We-Work/General-Information/Grant-Opportunities), while a lesser-known resource might be the Foundation for Rural Education Development (http://www.fred.org/tech.html).
  ★ The George Lucas Educational Foundation confers grants and also maintains an informational webpage with supports to help schools and teachers in identifying grant opportunities and developing grant proposals (http://www.edutopia.org/grant-information-resources-to-get-you-started).
  ★ Grant resources are constantly changing. To find out what grant, scholarship, and other opportunities are available, Internet searches are helpful, and again, universities with experienced researchers and grant writers may be uniquely positioned to help schools match opportunities to their needs.
★ Schools in suburban and wealthier areas may be willing to donate used but still functional equipment during their more frequent upgrades.

★ As an example, in Sarasota, Florida, the local education foundation partnered with the local school district to coordinate monetary and product donations to increase technology access and integration in their schools (http://www.sarasotacountyschools .net/departments/texcellence/default.aspx?id=4234). Boston Public Schools has a technology donation program too (http://www.bostonpublicschools.org/make-donation), as does the state of Delaware (http://www.dcet.k12.de.us/partech/).

★ Many districts and schools are implementing a *bring your own device* (BYOD) policy; however, for children at risk, the disparities in connectivity and access must be considered in making a policy.

Finding resources for technology can take time but can reap rich rewards for schools, teachers, and students. Few schools all by themselves have adequate internal resources to stay current. The above resources, hopefully, provide districts, schools, and teachers with a place to start finding partners to help them reach their technology goals.

CHAPTER SUMMARY

Technology is here to stay, and in order for children at risk to compete in our digital and global society, they need extensive access to well-integrated and diverse technologies and exposure to expert technology users. For schools and teachers, these are lofty objectives. Recruiting support from external sources such as universities, corporations, foundations, and within their communities is a must. Furthermore, development and membership within communities of practice and participation in professional development activities are needed for sustainable use and continuous growth. Technology changes rapidly, and schools and teachers face the challenge of keeping up to best serve children at risk who have among the highest needs and may stand to benefit the most from technology learning.

8 Collaborate With Other Professionals and Support Family Involvement

It is important for teachers to understand the resources that are available in schools. Yet in research we have conducted in Missouri, general educators did not know who was available to support children with social behavior needs, and many could not identify professionals who could conduct functional behavior assessments for children (e.g., school psychologists; Stormont, Reinke, & Herman, 2011b). This chapter outlines who is trained to provide different types of supports for children. The chapter also includes information on increasing family involvement and understanding the importance of increased collaborative efforts for families of children at risk.

Who is a good resource for assisting with academic or social behavior supports? Depending on the students' needs, the following people could be consulted for academic supports:

★ Reading specialist, if the problem relates to language or reading.
★ Speech pathologist, if the problem relates to language.
★ School psychologist, often a good resource for all topics addressed in this book. They also have skills in more intensive academic and

social behavior interventions for children who may need either more support or a referral for evaluation for special education and related services.

★ Behavior specialist or consultant, if the problem is behavioral. They, as with school psychologists, have skills related to assessing and determining additional perhaps more individualized support needs.

★ School counselor, if the problem is related to something currently happening in the family that is increasing risk for the student. Also, many school counselors are trained in evidence-based practices for supporting children with social emotional needs.

★ The assistive technology specialist, to identify appropriate assistive technology for children with disabilities. This evaluation should occur as part of the Individualized Education Program (IEP) process.

★ The school or district instructional/educational technology professional, the library/media specialist, and the special education teacher may have specialized knowledge about technologies and devices appropriate for children at risk.

★ Other teachers are good resources for supporting children if they have had success with using particular strategies in the past and/or if they have had professional development in specific areas.

★ Response-to-intervention teams. As more and more schools are using tiered systems of support to determine the level of support and resources different children (and adults) need, these teams are often invaluable resources. Response-to-intervention academic teams are those who support systematic screening and intervention options for children with reading or mathematics problems (Stormont, Reinke, Herman, & Lembke, 2012).

★ Families. The following section includes information on the importance of family involvement and strategies for increasing involvement (Adams & Christenson, 2000; Berger, 2000).

FAMILY INVOLVEMENT RESEARCH

Extensive research has been conducted on family involvement in children's education in school and at home.

★ When parents are involved in their children's education, there are benefits for both parents and children.

★ Involved parents feel better about their parenting, their ability to support their children's learning at home, and their relationships with teachers (Epstein 1995; Jackson & Davis, 2000).

★ Parent involvement lowers children's risk for many negative out-
comes, including later use of drugs and alcohol and dropping
out of school (Dearing, Kreider, Simpkins, & Weiss, 2006; Esler,
Godber, & Christenson, 2002; Fan & Chen, 2001; Hill & Craft, 2003;
International Reading Association, 2002; National Middle School
Association, 2003).

★ When children have involved parents, they are more likely to have
needed academic and social-emotional skills that allow them to
enter kindergarten ready for school and are more likely to be successful in kindergarten (Aikens & Barbarin, 2008; Dearing et al.,
2006; Mantzicopoulos, 2003; Stormont, Beckner, Mitchell, & Richter,
2005).

★ Teacher and school characteristics (supportiveness, biases toward
certain groups) influence how comfortable parents feel about
becoming involved (Stormont, Herman, Reinke, David, & Goel, in
press).

★ There are many ways families can be involved, and schools need
to consider how to increase involvement in flexible ways (Epstein,
1995; Turnbull, Turnbull, Erwin, Soodak, & Shogren, 2011).

★ Today, even when two parents are present in families, in the majority of cases, they both are working (Children's Defense Fund, 2008).
This is only one of the barriers to involvement; other reported challenges families face include work stress, parent stress, managing
basic needs, and taking care of housework (McWayne, Hampton,
Fantuzzo, Cohen, & Sekino, 2004).

★ Children at risk for failure may need more targeted efforts to
increase their families' involvement (Kaminski, Stormshak, Good, &
Goodman, 2002).

★ Increased family involvement also has positive outcomes for
schools, including higher teacher morale and community support
(Henderson & Mapp, 2002; Heymann & Earle, 2000).

Supporting Family Involvement

Knowing Yourself. Today's classrooms are increasingly diverse, and
teachers and their students often come from very different backgrounds
(Sleeter, 2008). Our own backgrounds, experiences, and beliefs strongly
influence our values about education and learning. We all have biases,
and it is important for teachers to know themselves well in order to work
effectively with diverse learners. Many teachers unintentionally harbor
some deficit thinking about common characteristics of children at risk,
such as poverty or cultural values (Harry & Klingner, 2007). Cross-cultural
competence requires self-awareness and a genuine interest in the beliefs
and values of others, especially when those differ significantly from our
own. Respecting children and families seems like a core value of education

and teachers, but because we are all human and individual, many school situations challenge teachers' ethics and actions. For example, how would teacher-family relationships be influenced for a teacher whose religion has a strong stance on sexuality yet has a child in his class with two mothers? Or a teacher from a very patriarchal background who has a child in her class whose cultural traditions are matriarchal? Or for the teacher who was raised in a home and is raising her own children to speak and sit quietly yet has a highly active young African American male in her classroom who uses a big voice and big movements to communicate (Webb-Johnson, 2003).

Many organizations provide materials for improving cross-cultural competence, including the National Education Association's Diversity Toolkit (http://www.nea.org/tools/30402.htm), The Equity Alliance (http://www.equityallianceatasu.org), Teaching Tolerance (http://www .tolerance.org), and Colorín Colorado (http://www.colorincolorado.org) to name a few. Project Implicit offers an online test to help interested individuals uncover hidden biases, with the intention of helping people make positive personal change (available at http://www.tolerance.org/ supplement/test-yourself-hidden-bias and http://www.projectimplicit .net/index.html).

In reading each of the following sections, teachers can reflect on themselves, their backgrounds, and their beliefs to consider how they are similar to or different from students and families they have known. Learning about our students is critical not only to their success but also to our own personal and professional growth.

Know Families. The first thing teachers can do to support family involvement is to know who is included in a child's family. The family may include extended family, close friends, cousins, and other people besides the nuclear family. It is also important to know families to understand who is available to support children's learning at home. Perhaps a grandparent watches a child several days a week and is available and willing to support extra practice in specific areas and literacy.

Another important consideration for teachers is that families are extremely busy trying to meet all the needs of family members. Education is only one of the needs families are trying to meet (Turnbull et al., 2011). It is very important for teachers to know if families are struggling to meet their day-to-day needs. If families are on the brink of homelessness or struggling with a serious illness or issue in the family, completing homework may fall by the wayside. It is important for teachers to be prepared to support families in meeting their basic needs by having knowledge of community agencies and school resources. If teachers support families' needs for support, this is an avenue to build a trusting relationship where families feel teachers really care about their success in supporting their child (Turnbull et al., 2011).

Positive, Respectful Communication. The way teachers can get to know families is through positive, respectful communication. Especially for children at risk for failure, the communication with families needs to be positive to support positive interactions between teachers and families in order to provide support for growth across settings.

As illustrated in Figure 8.1, to foster resilience and change the other environmental risk factors that children at risk may face in their homes (e.g., limited support for learning), teachers must be committed to trying to interact with families in positive ways. Families of children at risk for failure are also at risk for having more negative contacts with teachers as well as having teachers who feel less comfortable with families' involvement (Stormont et al., in press). Teachers need to make a strong effort to switch the pattern of contact with families of children at risk that has been documented in research. The manner in which this can be accomplished is by tracking every contact made with families and coding whether the contact was positive or negative (see example below and blank communication log in Table 8.1). Then teachers can be mindful of the need to have positive contacts with all families but especially with the ones with whom

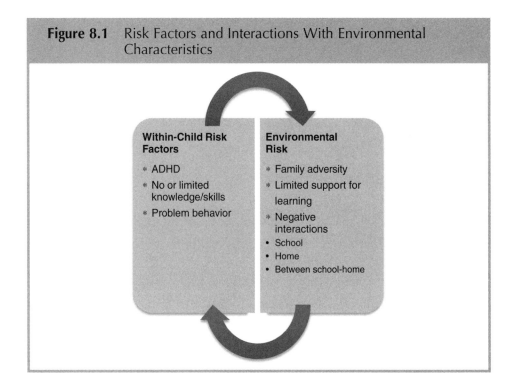

Figure 8.1 Risk Factors and Interactions With Environmental Characteristics

Within-Child Risk Factors

* ADHD
* No or limited knowledge/skills
* Problem behavior

Environmental Risk

* Family adversity
* Limited support for learning
* Negative interactions
• School
• Home
• Between school-home

they have had a negative contact. Regardless of how kind teachers are when delivering "bad news" about their child, it is most often stressful for families to receive this information. Therefore, receiving information on when children excel at something, have a good day, or just make a kind gesture can help families feel more comfortable in their communication with educators.

Communication Log: Ratio of Positive to Negative Contacts

Who?	What? How?	When?	Nature + or–
Anthony	Homework not being completed—*e-mail*	1/25	–
Samantha	Tardiness—*e-mail*	1/26	–
Samantha	Being on time—*left phone message*	1/27	+
Anthony	Homework completed—*e-mail*	2/5	+
Anthony	Beat his former time by 1 minute on multiplication facts—*left phone message*	2/10	+

Foster Trust. If families believe that educators are working to support their children's best interests, then trust is present. People have different dispositions about trust, based on their personal traits and their history with other people (Turnbull et al., 2011). Strategies for increasing the likelihood that trust will form include knowing families and positive communication as discussed above. Additional strategies for forming trusting relationships include being respectful, honoring cultural diversity, being committed, and being competent (Turnbull et al., 2011). Teachers need to be open to things that are important to families, even if they seem to interfere with educational tasks. They also need to be confidential with family and student information at all times. Teachers also need to demonstrate that they are committed to learning about ways to be a better teacher at all times. When teachers do not know the answer to a question, they need to be honest and then demonstrate they want to find out. All teachers should have a little notebook or log of some sort that is a specific database on what they told people they would do. It could be called a Trust Me Log, and it would include the names of families and professionals and what the teacher said he or she would do. Sometimes simple follow-through can

Table 8.1 Communication Log: Ratio of Positive to Negative Contacts

Who?	What?	When?	Nature + or–

create a context where increased trust can occur. An example follows, and Table 8.2 includes a blank form.

Trust Me Log

Who?	What?	When?	Follow Up?
Mrs. Miller	I would look into eligibility for a scholarship for girls on the run	January 2, 2013	January 4, called and told her I had left a message and the director would get back with me. January 6, called with scholarship application details

Plans to Increase Family Involvement

Children at risk for failure due to poverty are at risk for having less parental contact with schools (Aikens & Barbarin, 2008; Dearing et al., 2008). Unfortunately, children at risk due to low incomes may have teachers with negative opinions of their families' efforts toward their education; research has found that teachers in high-achieving low-income schools have more positive perceptions of parents and are more encouraging of families' involvement compared with teachers in less successful schools (McCoach et al., 2010). Families of children at risk may also feel schools are less welcoming and may avoid contact because of this perception (McCoach et al., 2010; Stormshak, Dishion, Light, & Yasui, 2005; Walker, Ice, Hoover-Dempsey, & Sandler, 2011).

Thus, it is critical that specific targeted efforts to increase family involvement in ways that fit families' resources and preferences are made by schools and teachers. Understanding and overcoming barriers to contact with schools, such as the need for child care or transportation, is another critical way to increase family involvement (McKay, Atkins, Hawkins, Brown, & Lynn, 2003; Nock & Kazdin, 2001). Families are more likely to be involved if they feel schools and teachers are welcoming and that what is being asked of them is acceptable and something they can actually do (McCoach et al., 2010; Walker et al., 2011).

To this end, teachers should develop focused plans to increase family involvement. First, teachers should reflect on the following questions:

★ Are there families that you believe aren't as involved as they could be in their child's education?
★ What are some reasons you think families may not be involved?
★ What are some barriers to family involvement in children's education at home and at school?

Table 8.2 Trust Me Log

Who?	What?	When?	Follow Up?

★ Do you have any biases that you think may serve as a barrier for family involvement? If yes, how can you overcome these barriers?
★ What are some specific things you can do that will increase family involvement in school?
★ How are you going to collect data on your efforts to increase family involvement?

These questions are also included in a family reflection questionnaire in Figure 8.2. Then, teachers can develop a professional plan to improve parent involvement. The following examples illustrate how teachers can target areas, develop goals, and monitor progress. Figure 8.2 has a blank form that teachers can complete.

Example 1: Increasing Family Involvement

Target for Improvement	Specific Goal	Monitor Progress	Additional Considerations
Increase amount of positive contacts with families early in the year.	Have at least two positive contacts with each family in the first two months of school.	Log names of students and number of positive and negative contacts.	If negative contact occurs, quickly have two positive contacts on students' progress.[a]

[a]Over time, we want to strive to have many more positive contacts than negative.

Example 2: Increasing Family Involvement

Target for Improvement	Specific Goal	Monitor Progress	Additional Considerations
Increase outreach efforts by knowing families.	Know families who are struggling to meet basic needs and match them with resources.	Develop community resource lists and keep track of the number of families connected to resources.	Provide different types of outreach for families (phone calls, visit on weekends or times convenient for family).

Example 3: Increasing Family Involvement

Target for Improvement	Specific Goal	Monitor Progress	Additional Considerations
Increase knowledge of barriers to involvement.	Ask families to complete a brief questionnaire on barriers at the beginning of the year.	Determine barriers for specific families and make a plan to overcome specific barriers.	Target a few barriers at a time, such as work schedule conflicts = making calls on the weekend instead of meeting at school.

Figure 8.2 Reflection on Family Involvement and Professional Development Plan

Are there families that you believe aren't as involved as they could be in their child's education?

What are some reasons you think families may not be involved?

What are some barriers to family involvement in children's education at home and at school?

Do you have any biases that you think may serve as a barrier for family involvement? If yes, how can you overcome these barriers?

What are some specific things you can do that will increase family involvement in school?

How are you going to collect data on your efforts to increase family involvement?

(Continued)

Figure 8.2 (Continued)

Complete the following plan for increasing family involvement:

Target(s) for Improvement	Specific Goal	Monitor Progress	Additional Considerations

Example 4: Increasing Family Involvement

Target for Improvement	Specific Goal	Monitor Progress	Additional Considerations
Increase cultural sensitivity.	Get to know cultural influences for children by targeting specific cultures present in schools.	Determine readings to assist and discuss cultural preferences with families.	It is important to be sensitive but not stereotypic; each family is different.

Connecting Families to Resources

It is also vital that schools connect families who need specific supports to relevant resources in the community. For example, teachers can work with counselors and other school professionals to determine needs of children and families in school. Children may need resources such as dental care, immunizations, clothes, shoes, ways to get food over the weekend and in the summer, and places that provide free afterschool activities.

CHAPTER SUMMARY

The focus of this chapter was to both highlight the importance of collaboration with families and professionals as well as to provide specific examples of professionals who can assist teachers when working with children at risk. Main points include the following:

★ There are often many professionals available in schools to support teachers in their work with children at risk for failure in schools.
★ Family involvement is highly associated with success in schools.
★ It is imperative that educators demonstrate commitment to trying to increase family involvement through thoughtful reflection and systematic efforts.

Appendix

Description and Access Information for Educational Technology Resources Cited

Resource	Reference	Description	URL
ArtikPix	Chapter 4 Page 40	This app includes flashcard and matching activities for children with speech and language delays to improve articulation. Data collection capabilities are built in.	http://ericsailers .com/artikpix.html
Behavior Tracker Pro	Chapter 3 Page 35	This app helps teachers and others to track and graph behavior as part of assessment and intervention.	http://www .behaviortrackerpro .com
Center for Applied Special Technology (CAST)	Chapter 6 Page 64 Chapter 7 Page 79	CAST is a research and development organization that conceptualized Universal Design for Learning (UDL). This website provides background, information, and resources to support educators in understanding and implementing UDL.	http://www.cast .org
Center for Effective Collaboration and Practice (CECP)	Chapter 5 Page 58	CECP is an organization whose mission is to provide resources to support quality education for children with and at risk for emotional and behavioral disorders. A wealth of resources for prevention, assessment, and	http://cecp .air.org/fba/ problembehavior3/ appendixc.htm

Resource	Reference	Description	URL
		intervention are offered, including the Forced-Choice Reinforcement Inventory referenced in this book.	
Developmental Reading Assessement— 2nd Edition PLUS	Chapter 3 Page 23	DRA2+ is a criterion-referenced formative assessment tool that includes automatic scoring features and views of ongoing student progress to help teachers evaluate reading performance and improve instruction.	http://www .pearsonschool .com/index.cfm?lo cator=PSZw5u&P MDbSiteId=2781&P MDbSolutionId=67 24&PMDbSubSolu tionId=&PMDbCat egoryId=3289&PM DbSubCategoryId= 28139&PMDbSubje ctAreaId=&PMDbP rogramId=23661
edHelper	Chapter 6 Page 66	edHelper is a teacher developed website designed to provide access to educational resources, including the graphic organizers offered in this text.	http://www .edhelper.com
Education Place	Chapter 6 Page 66	Education Place, sponsored by educational publishing company Houghton Mifflin Harcourt, offers web-based textbook supports for grades pre-K to 6, such as graphic organizers suggested in this book.	http://www .eduplace.com
Edudemic	Chapter 3 Page 30	Edudemic is an education technology news site with a goal of connecting educators to technology.	http://www .edudemic.com
Edutopia	Chapter 7 Page 84	Edutopia, the website of the George Lucas Educational Foundation, has a mission to promote and improve access to evidence-based educational resources. Resources are offered by grade level and for a variety of topics and	http://www .edutopia.org/ grant-information-resources-to-get-you-started

Resource	Reference	Description	URL
		include professional development. While the George Lucas Educational Foundation does not offer grants, the website does provide a resource list to help teachers and others identify avenues of support.	
flashcard apps	Chapter 4 Page 39	This website was created by the app developer of Vocabulary Ninja (http://www.vocabninja.com) to document the features of all similar apps. Realizing it might be helpful to others, she has hosted this resource.	http://www.flashcardapps.info/filter/srs-plus/
Free Rice	Chapter 4 Page 40	Free Rice is an online vocabulary game that asks players to identify the best synonym for each word presented. It was developed by the United Nations World Food Program and has a social justice mission with 10 grains of rice donated toward hunger relief for each correct answer.	http://freerice.com/#/english-vocabulary/1517
Holt Interactive Graphic Organizers	Chapter 6 Page 66	This resource is provided by Holt McDougal, an affiliate of educational publisher Houghton Mifflin and Harcourt. This web link offers access to a wide variety of interactive graphic organizers	http://my.hrw.com/nsmedia/intgos/html/igo.htm
Intervention Central	Chapter 3 Page 27 Chapter 5 Page 58	This website was created by a school psychologist and educational consultant to provide intervention and assessment resources for Grades K–12.	http://www.interventioncentral.org
Jackpot! Reinforcement Survey Generator	Chapter 5 Page 58	This web-based survey generator is offered at Intervention Central.	http://www.jimwrightonline.com/php/jackpot/jackpot.php

Resource	Reference	Description	URL
Kid Coach: The KidTools Support System	Chapter 3 Page 35 Chapter 6 Page 74	This website offers research-based tools, templates, and strategies to support students in self-management for learning, behavior, and problem solving to improve school success.	http://kidtools.org
National Center on Accessible Instructional Materials	Chapter 7 Page 77	This website provides information and resources for Accessible Instructional Materials, specialized formats of curriculum to provide access to education for students with print disabilities.	http://aim.cast.org
National Center on Universal Design for Learning	Chapter 7 Page 80	The National Center on UDL supports the effective implementation of UDL by providing information and resources for UDL advocacy, research, development, and implementation.	http://www .udlcenter.org
National Library of Virtual Manipulatives	Chapter 4 Page 39	The National Library of Virtual Manipulatives, supported by the National Science Foundation, offers a library of interactive virtual manipulatives and concept tutorials to support K–12 mathematics learning.	http://nlvm.usu .edu/en/nav/ vlibrary.html
Percentally	Chapter 3 Page 35	Percentally is a data collection app that uses tallies and total to calculate percentage correct. This tool is useful for progress monitoring rate and accuracy of a given behavior.	http://ericsailers .com/percentally .html
Preference and Reinforcer Assessment	Chapter 5 Page 58	This app, designed by a Board Certified Behavior Analyst, helps teachers identify effective and appropriate reinforcers based on student choice.	https://itunes .apple.com/us/ app/preference-reinforcer-assessment/ id436692530?mt=8

Resource	Reference	Description	URL
Reading Rockets	Chapter 3 Page 28 and 30	A service of WETA, Washington's major public broadcasting channel and is largely funded by the U.S. Department of Education, Office of Special Education Programs, Reading Rockets offers research-based strategies to help teachers and families support reading development.	http://www .readingrockets.org
readwritethink	Chapter 3 Page 30	This website, supported by the International Reading Association, the National Council of English Teachers, and Verizon's Thinkfinity, provides educators and families with access to high-quality instructional materials for language arts.	http://www .readwritethink.org
STAR Reading	Chapter 3 Page 23	STAR Reading, from Renaissance Learning, a technology-based educational company, is an online resource that uses skills-based assessments to help teachers screen, benchmark, plan for instruction, and monitor reading progress.	http://www .renlearn.com/sr/
Starfall	Chapter 4 Page 39	Starfall is the creation of a former struggling reader. This website offers interactive activities for young readers who need practice in phonemic awareness, decoding, and fluency.	http://www .starfall .com
Technical Assistance Center on Positive Behavior Interventions and Supports	Chapter 5 Page 52	This website, sponsored by the Office of Special Education Programs, provides information, resources, and technical support to promote wide-scale implementation of	www.pbis.org

Resource	Reference	Description	URL
		the positive behavior interventions and supports (PBIS) model.	
Technology Integration for Teachers	Chapter 4 Page 39	This website is hosted by an instructional technology coordinator from Chicago who has gathered a quantity of web-based resources for K–8 teachers. It is organized by content area and includes tips, resources, and apps lists for specific devices.	http://www .techforteachers .net/apps— math-practice.html
Time Timer	Chapter 3 Page 25	This app was designed by a mother who wanted to make the concept of elapsing time visual yet simple. Time timer comes in clock-, watch-, and device-based formats and can be set in second and minutes; some products come with languages in addition to English.	http://www .timetimer.com
Wordle	Chapter 2 Page 14 Chapter 7 Page 82	Wordle is a free online tool that creates word clouds from text that is entered by a user. It is partially owned by IBM, and its developer has described it as a toy. However, many educators have identified educational uses for Wordle to meet instructional objectives.	http://www .wordle .net
Wordsift	Chapter 7 Page 82	Wordsift is a free online tool to help teachers support the development of content vocabulary in academic disciplines. This tool was developed through a partnership between teachers and university researchers. Learning theory regarding vocabulary development and English language acquisition, and research on previewing of vocabulary for content area comprehension were used to guide development.	http://www .wordsift.com

References

Adams, K. S., & Christenson, S. L. (2000). Trust and the family-school relationship examination of parent-teacher differences in elementary and secondary grades. *Journal of School Psychology, 38*(5), 477–497.

Aikens, N. L., & Barbarin, O. (2008). Socioeconomic differences in reading trajectories: The contribution of family, neighborhood, and school contexts. *Journal of Educational Psychology, 100,* 235–251.

Alberto, P. A., & Troutman, A. C. (2011). *Applied behavior analysis for teachers* (9th ed.). Englewood Cliffs, NJ: Prentice Hall.

Archer, A., & Gleason, M. (1993). *Skills for school success series.* Billerica, MT: Curriculum Associates.

Assistive Technology Act of 2004, 29 U.S.C. § 2202(2) (October 25, 2004).

Atkins, D., Bennett, J., Brown, J. S., Chopra, A., Dede, C., Fishman, B., . . . Williams, B. (2010). *Transforming American education: Learning powered by technology.* National Educational Technology Plan 2010. Washington, DC: U.S. Department of Education, Office of Educational Technology.

Aziz, H. (2010). The 5 keys to educational technology. *T.H.E Journal.* Retrieved from http://thejournal.com/articles/2010/09/16/the-5-keys-to-educational-technology .aspx

Barkley, R. (1995). *Taking charge of ADHD: The complete authoritative guide for parents.* New York, NY: Guilford Press.

Barkley, R. (2006). *Attention-deficit hyperactivity disorder: A handbook for diagnosis and treatment* (3rd ed.). New York, NY: Guilford Press.

Belfiore, P. J., Auld, R., & Lee, D. L. (2005). The disconnection of poor-urban education: Equal access and a pedagogy of risk taking. *Psychology in the Schools, 42,* 855–863.

Berger, E. H. (2000). *Parents as partners in education: Families and schools working together* (5th ed.). Upper Saddle River, NJ: Merrill Prentice Hall.

Bess, S. (1994). *Nobody don't love nobody: Lessons in love from the school with no name.* Carson City, NV: Gold Leaf Press.

Bouck, E. C., & Flanagan, S. M. (2009). Virtual manipulatives: What they are and how teachers can use them. *Intervention in School and Clinic, 45*(3), 186–191.

Brawley, S., & Stormont, M. (in press). Investigating reported data practices in early childhood: An exploratory study. *Journal of Positive Behavior Interventions.*

Burns, M. K., Griffiths, A., Parson, L. B., Tilly, W. D., & VanderHayden, A. (2007). *Response to intervention: Research for practice.* Alexandria, VA: National Association of State Directors of Special Education.

Cartwright, C. A., & Cartwright, G. P. (1970). Determining the motivational systems of individual children. *Teaching Exceptional Children, 2*(3), 143–149.

Children's Defense Fund. (2008). *The state of America's children.* Retrieved from http:// www.childrensdefense.org/child-research-data-publications/data/state-of-americas-children-2008-report.html

Clark, R. E. (1994). Media and method. *Educational Technology Research & Development, 42*(3), 7–10.

Conroy, M., Sutherland, K., Haydon, T., Stormont, M., & Harmon, J. (2009). Preventing and ameliorating young children's chronic problem behaviors: An ecological classroom-based approach. *Psychology in the Schools, 46,* 3–17.

Copple, C., & Bredekamp, S. (2009). *Developmentally appropriate practice in early childhood programs serving children from birth through age 8* (3rd ed.). Washington, DC: National Association for the Education of Young Children.

Coyne, M. D., Kame'enui, E. J., & Carnine, D. W. (2011). *Effective teaching strategies that accommodate diverse learners* (4th ed.). Boston, MA: Pearson.

Cuban, L., Kirkpatrick, H., & Peck, C. (2001). High access and low use of technologies in high school classrooms: Explaining an apparent paradox. *American Educational Research Journal, 38*(4), 813–834.

Dalton, J., & Watson, M. (1997). *Among friends: Classrooms where caring and learning prevail.* Oakland, CA: Developmental Studies Center.

Darney, D., Reinke, W. M., Herman, K. C., Stormont, M., & Ialongo, N. (2013). Children with co-occurring academic and behavior problems in 1st grade: Distal outcomes in 12th grade. *Journal of School Psychology, 51*(1), 117–128.

Dearing, E., Kreider, H., Simpkins, S., & Weiss, H. B. (2006). Family involvement in school and low-income children's literacy: Longitudinal associations between and within families. *Journal of Educational Psychology, 98,* 653–664.

Edyburn, D. (2007). What every teacher needs to know about special education technology. *Special Education Technology Practice, 9*(1), 17–25.

Epstein, J. L. (1995, May). School/family/community partnerships. *Phi Delta Kappan, 76,* 702–712.

Esler, A. N., Godber, Y., & Christenson, S. L. (2002). Best practices in supporting home-school collaboration. In A. Thomas & J. Grimes (Eds.), *Best practices in school psychology IV* (Vol. 1, pp. 389–411). Bethesda, MD: National Association of School Psychologists.

Espinosa, L. M. (2005). Curriculum and assessment considerations for young children from culturally, linguistically, and economically diverse backgrounds. *Psychology in the Schools, 42,* 837–853.

Fan, X. T., & Chen, M. (2001). Parental involvement and students' academic achievement: A meta-analysis. *Educational Psychology Review, 13,* 1–22.

Gable, R. A. (1991). *Forced-choice reinforcement menu.* Center for Effective Collaboration and Practice. Retrieved from http://cecp.air.org/fba/problembehavior3/appendixc.htm

Gibson, J. J. (1977). The theory of affordances. In R. Shaw & J. D. Bransford (Eds.), *Perceiving, acting, and knowing* (pp. 67–82). Hillsdale, NJ: Lawrence Erlbaum.

Harry, B., & Klingner, J. K. (2007). Discarding the deficit model. *Educational Leadership, 64*(5), 16–21.

Henderson, A. T., & Mapp, K. L. (2002). *A new wave of evidence: The impact of school, family, and community connections on student achievement.* Austin, TX: National Center for Family and Community Connections with Schools.

Herman, K. C., Reinke, W. M., Stormont, M., Puri, R., & Agarwal, G. (2010). Using prevention science to promote children's mental health: The founding of the Missouri Prevention Center. *The Counseling Psychologist, 38,* 652–690.

Heymann, S. J., & Earle, A. (2000). Low-income parents: How do working conditions affect their opportunity to help school-age children at risk? *American Educational Research Journal, 37,* 833–848.

Hill, N. E., & Craft, S. A. (2003). Parent-school involvement and school performance: Mediated pathways among socioeconomically comparable African-American and Euro-American families. *Journal of Educational Psychology, 95,* 74–83.

Hoagwood, K., Olin, S., Kerker, B., Kratochwill, T., Crowe, M., & Saka, N. (2007). Empirically based school interventions targeted at academic and mental health functioning. *Journal of Emotional and Behavioral Disorders, 15,* 66–92.

International Reading Association. (2002). *Family-school partnerships: Essential elements of literacy instruction in the United States.* A position statement of the International Reading Association. Newark, DE: Author.

Jackson, A., & Davis, P. G. (2000). *Turning points 2000: Educating adolescents in the 21st century.* New York, NY: Teachers College Press.

Jonassen, D. H., Reeves, T. C., Hong, N., Harvey, D., & Peters, K. (1997). Concept mapping as cognitive learning and assessment tools. *Journal of Interactive Learning Research, 8*(3), 289–308.

Jones, V. F., & Jones, L. S. (2001). *Comprehensive classroom management: Creating communities of support and solving problems.* Boston, MA: Allyn & Bacon.

Kaminski, R. A., Stormshak, E. A., Good, R. H., & Goodman, M. R. (2002). Prevention of substance abuse with rural Head Start children and families: Results of Project STAR. *Psychology of Addictive Behaviors, 16,* S11–S26.

Kauffman, J. M., & Landrum, T. J. (2009). *Characteristics of emotional and behavioral disorders of children and youth.* Upper Saddle River, NJ: Merrill/Pearson.

Lehr, C. A., & Christenson, S. L. (2002). Best practices in promoting a positive school climate. In A. Thomas & G. Grimes (Eds.), *Best practices in school psychology IV* (Vol. 1, pp. 929–948). Bethesda, MD: National Association of School Psychologists.

Mantzicopoulos, P. (2003). Flunking kindergarten after Head Start: An inquiry into the contribution of contextual and individual variables. *Journal of Educational Psychology, 95,* 268–278.

McArthur Capizzi, A., & Barton-Arwood, S. M. (2009). Using a curriculum-based measurement graphic organizer to facilitate collaboration in reading. *Intervention in School and Clinic, 45*(1), 14–23.

McCoach, D., Goldstein, J., Behuniak, P., Reis, S. M., Black, A. C., Sullivan, E. E., & Rambo, K. (2010). Examining the unexpected: Outlier analyses of factors affecting student achievement. *Journal of Advanced Academics, 21,* 426–468.

McKay, M. M., Atkins, M. S., Hawkins, T., Brown, C., & Lynn, C. J. (2003). Inner-city African American parental involvement in children's schooling: Racial socialization and social support from the parent community. *American Journal of Community Psychology, 32,* 107–114.

McWayne, C., Hampton, V., Fantuzzo, J., Cohen, H. L., & Sekino, Y. (2004). A multivariate examination of parent involvement and the social and academic competencies of urban kindergarten children. *Psychology in the Schools, 41*(3), 363–377.

Miller, K. J., Fitzgerald, G. E., Koury, K. A., Mitchem, K.J., & Hollingsead, C. (2007). KidTools: Self-management, problem-solving, organizational, and planning software for children and teachers. *Intervention in School and Clinic, 43*(1), 12–19. doi: 10.1177/10534512070430010201

Mitschelen, K. (2013). *Upper elementary community-building classroom activities.* Retrieved from http://voices.yahoo.com/upper-elementary-community-building-classroom-activities-2129708.html?cat=4

Moore, J. L., Laffey, J. M., Espinosa, L. M., & Lodree, A. W. (2002). Bridging the digital divide for at-risk students. *TechTrends, 46*(2), 4–9.

National Center on Family Homelessness. (2011). *The characteristics and needs of families experiencing homelessness.* Retrieved from http://www.familyhomelessness.org/media/306.pdf

National Center on Universal Design for Learning. (2012a). About UDL. Retrieved from http://www.udlcenter.org/aboutudl/whatisudl

National Center on Universal Design for Learning. (2012b). UDL guidelines—Version 2.0. Retrieved from http://www.udlcenter.org/aboutudl/udlguidelines

National Coalition for the Homeless. (2009). *Why are people homeless?* Retrieved from http://www.nationalhomeless.org/factsheets/why.html

National Council of Teachers of English. (2013). *Read, write, think: Strategy guide exit slips.* Retrieved from http://www.readwritethink.org/professional-development/strategy-guides/exit-slips-30760.html

National Institute of Child Health and Human Development. (2000). *Report of the National Reading Panel. Teaching children to read: An evidence-based assessment of the scientific research literature on reading and its implications for reading instruction* (NIH Publication No. 00–4769). Washington, DC: Government Printing Office.

National Middle School Association. (2003). *This we believe: Successful schools for young adolescents.* Westerville, OH: Author.

Nock, M. K., & Kazdin, A. E. (2001). Parent expectancies for child therapy: Assessment and relation to participation in treatment. *Journal of Child and Family Studies, 10,* 155–180.

Paquette, K. (2011). Families experiencing homelessness. Fact sheet from the Homelessness Resource Center. Retrieved from http://homeless.samhsa.gov/Resource/View.aspx?id=48806

Pianta, R. C. (1999). *Enhancing relationships between children and teachers: School psychology book series.* Washington, DC: American Psychological Association.

Pianta, R. C., & Walsh, D. J. (1998). Applying the construct of resilience in schools: Cautions from a developmental systems perspective. *School Psychology Review, 27,* 407–417.

Raskind, M., & Bryant, B. R. (2002). *FEAT: Functional assessment for assistive technology.* Austin, TX: Pro-Ed.

Reinke, W., Stormont, M., Herman, K. C., Puri, R., & Goel, N. (2011). Supporting children's mental health in schools: Teacher perceptions of needs, roles, and barriers. *School Psychology Quarterly, 26,* 1–13.

Reinke, W. M., Herman, K. C., Petras, H., & Ialongo, N. S. (2008). Empirically derived subtypes of child academic and behavior problems: Co-occurrence and distal outcomes. *Journal of Abnormal Child Psychology, 36*(5), 759–770.

Rieth, H. J., Bryant, D. P., Kinzer, C. K., Colburn, L. K., Hur, S., Hartman, P., & Choi, H. S. (2003). An analysis of the impact of anchored instruction on teaching and learning activities in two ninth-grade language arts classes. *Remedial and Special Education, 24*(3), 173–184.

Rones, M., & Hoagwood, K. (2000). School-based mental health services: A research review. *Clinical Child and Family Psychology Review, 3,* 223–241.

Skinner, C. H., Cashwell, T. H., & Skinner, A. L. (2000). Increasing tootling: The effects of a peer-monitored group contingency program on students' reports of peers' prosocial behaviors. *Psychology in the Schools, 37,* 263–270.

Sleeter, C. E. (2008). Preparing white teachers for diverse students. In M. Cochran-Smith, F.-N. Sharon, & J. D. McIntyre (Eds.), *Handbook of research on teacher education: Enduring questions in changing contexts* (3rd ed., pp. 559–582). New York, NY: Routledge and Association of Teacher Educators.

Stormont, M. (2001). Social outcomes of children with AD/HD: Contributing factors and implications for practice. *Psychology in the Schools, 38,* 521–531.

Stormont, M. (2007). *Fostering resilience in young children at risk for failure: Strategies for K-3.* Upper Saddle River, NJ: Pearson.

Stormont, M. (2008). 20 ways to increase academic success for children with AD/HD using sticky notes and highlighters. *Intervention in School and Clinic, 43,* 305–308.

Stormont, M., Beckner, R., Mitchell, B., & Richter, M. (2005). Supporting successful transition to kindergarten: General challenges and specific implications for students with problem behavior. *Psychology in the Schools, 42*(8), 765–778.

Stormont, M., Herman, K. C., Reinke, W. M., David, K. B., & Goel, N. (in press). Latent profile analysis of teacher perceptions of parent contact and comfort. *School Psychology Quarterly.*

Stormont, M., Lewis, T. J., Beckner, R., & Johnson, N. W. (2008). *Implementing positive behavior support systems in early childhood and elementary settings.* Thousand Oaks, CA: Corwin.

Stormont, M. A., & McCathren, R. B. (in press). Nowhere to turn: The young face of homelessness. In D. Capuzzi & D. R. Gross (Eds.), *Youth at risk: Prevention resource for counselors, teachers, and parents* (6th ed.). Alexandria, VA: American Counseling Association.

Stormont, M., & Reinke, W. (2009). The importance of precorrection and specific behavioral praise and strategies to increase their use. *Beyond Behavior, 18*(3), 26–32.

Stormont, M., Reinke, W. M., & Herman, K. C. (2011a). Teacher characteristics and ratings for evidence-based behavior interventions. *Behavior Disorders, 37,* 19–29.

Stormont, M., Reinke, W. M., & Herman, K. C. (2011b). Teachers' knowledge of evidence-based interventions and available school resources for children with emotional or behavioral problems. *Journal of Behavioral Education, 20,* 138–147.

Stormont, M., Reinke, W., Herman, K., & Lembke, E. (2012). *Academic and behavior supports for at-risk students: Tier 2 interventions.* New York, NY: Guilford Press.

Stormont, M., & Stebbins, M. S. (2005). Preschool teachers' knowledge, opinions, and educational experiences related to attention deficit/hyperactivity disorder: An exploratory study. *Teacher Education and Special Education, 28*(1), 52–61.

Stormshak, E. A., Dishion, T. J., Light, J., & Yasui, M. (2005). Implementing family-centered interventions within the public middle school: Linking service delivery to change in student problem behavior. *Journal of Abnormal Child Psychology, 33,* 723–733.

Sugai, G. (2011). School-wide positive behavior support and response to intervention. Retrieved from http://www.rtinetwork.org/learn/behavior-supports/schoolwide-behavior

Thomas, C. N. (2007, April). Scatter plots and ABC charts: Two simple ways to make data-based decisions about challenging behavior. *LD Forum,* pp. 4–7.

Thomas, C. N., Hassaram, B., Rieth, H. J., Raghavan, N. S., Kinzer, C. K., & Mulloy, A. M. (2012). The Integrated Curriculum Project: Teacher change and student outcomes within a university-school professional development collaboration. *Psychology in the Schools, 49*(5), 444–464.

Torres-Velasquez, D., & Lobo, G. (2004–2005). Culturally responsive mathematics teaching and English language learners. *Teaching Children Mathematics, 11*(5), 249–255.

Turnbull, A., Turnbull, R., Erwin, E., Soodak, L., & Shogren, K. A. (2011). *Families, professionals, and exceptionality: Positive outcomes through partnership and trust* (6th ed.). Upper Saddle River, NJ: Pearson.

U.S. Census Bureau. (2012). *Income, poverty, and health insurance coverage in the United States: 2011.* Retrieved from http://www.census.gov/prod/2012pubs/p60–243.pdf

Vaughn, S., & Bos, C. S. (2009). *Strategies for teaching students with learning and behavior problems* (7th ed.). Boston, MA: Allyn & Bacon.

Walker, H. M., Ramsey, E., & Gresham, F. M. (2004). *Antisocial behavior in school: Evidence-based practices* (2nd ed.). Belmont, CA: Wadsworth/Thomson Learning.

Walker, J. T., Ice, C. L., Hoover-Dempsey, K. V., & Sandler, H. M. (2011). Latino parents' motivations for involvement in their children's schooling. *Elementary School Journal, 111,* 409–429.

Watson, M., & Ecken, L. (2003). *Learning to trust: Transforming difficult elementary classrooms through developmental discipline.* San Francisco, CA: Jossey-Bass.

Webb-Johnson, G. (2003). Behaving While Black: A hazardous reality for African American learners? *Beyond Behavior, 12*(2), 3–7.

Weinstein, C. S., & Mignano, A. J. (2003). *Elementary classroom management: Lessons from research and practice* (3rd ed.). New York, NY: McGraw-Hill.

Wright, J. (2010, December). *RTI: Teacher-friendly methods for tracking student progress: Packet 2.* Retrieved from http://www.jimwrightonline.com/mixed_files/sachem/wright_Data_Collection_Sachem_Schools_12_Jan_2011.pdf

World Health Organization. (2004). *Prevention of mental disorders: Effective interventions and policy options*. Summary report. Geneva, Switzerland: Author.

Zabala, J. (2010–2013). Sharing the SETT framework. Retrieved from http://www.joyzabala .com/Home.php

Zentall, S. S. (2005). Theory- and evidence-based strategies for children with attention problems. *Psychology in the Schools, 42,* 821–836.

Zentall, S. S. (2006). *ADHD and education: Foundations, characteristics, methods, and collaboration.* Upper Saddle River, NJ: Merrill/Prentice Hall.

Zentall, S. S., Harper, G. W., & Stormont-Spurgin, M. (1993). Children with hyperactivity and their organizational abilities. *Journal of Educational Research, 87*(2), 112–117.

Zorfass, J., & Rivero, H. K. (2005). Collaboration is key: How a community of practice promotes technology integration. *Journal of Special Education Technology, 20*(3), 51–67.

Index

CORWIN
A SAGE Company

The Corwin logo—a raven striding across an open book—represents the union of courage and learning. Corwin is committed to improving education for all learners by publishing books and other professional development resources for those serving the field of PreK–12 education. By providing practical, hands-on materials, Corwin continues to carry out the promise of its motto: **"Helping Educators Do Their Work Better."**